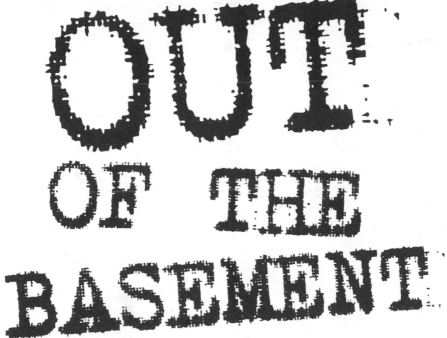

OUT OF THE BASEMENT

From Cheap Trick to DIY Punk in
Rockford, Illinois, 1973-2005

OUT OF THE BASEMENT

From Cheap Trick to DIY Punk in Rockford, Illinois, 1973-2005

David A Ensminger

MICROCOSM
Portland, OR

OUT OF THE BASEMENT
From Cheap Trick to DIY Punk in Rockford, IL 1973-2005

David A Ensminger

First printing, February 14, 2017
All text © David A Ensminger, 2017
This edition © by Microcosm Publishing, 2017

Microcosm Publishing
2752 N Williams Ave
Portland, OR 97227

Microcosm Publishing .com

Volume 3 in the *Scene History Series:*
#1: *Punk in NYC's Lower East Side 1981-1991*
#2: *Rock & Roll of San Francisco's East Bay, 1950-1980*
#3: *Out of the Basement: From Cheap Trick to DIY Punk in Rockford, Illinois, 1973-2005*
#4: *The Prodigal Rogerson: The Tragic, Hilarious, and Possibly Apocryphal Story of Circle Jerks Bassist Roger Rogerson in the Golden Age of LA Punk, 1979-2006 (May 2017)*

For a catalog, write or visit MicrocosmPublishing.com

ISBN 978-1-62106-766-5
This is Microcosm #219

Edited by Taylor Hurley and Joe Biel

Designed by Joe Biel

Distributed by Legato / Perseus Books Group and in the UK by Turnaround.

This book was printed on post-consumer paper in the United States.

You can contribute to future issues of the *Scene History Series*, our first open-submission project, by visiting Microcosmpublishing.com/scene-history

Library of Congress Cataloging-in-Publication Data

Names: Ensminger, David A.
Title: Out of the basement : from Cheap Trick to DIY punk in Rockford, Illinois, 1973-2005 / David A. Ensminger.
Description: Portland, OR : Microcosm Publishing, 2017.
Identifiers: LCCN 2016014332 (print) | LCCN 2016015914 (ebook) | ISBN 9781621067665 (trade pbk.) | ISBN 9781621065371 (epdf) | ISBN 9781621061236 (epub) | ISBN 9781621069492 (mobi)
Subjects: LCSH: Rock music—Illinois—Rockford—History and criticism. | Rock musicians—Illinois—Rockford. | Rockford (Ill.)—Social life and customs.
Classification: LCC ML3534.3 .E65 2017 (print) | LCC ML3534.3 (ebook) | DDC 781.6609773/31—dc23
LC record available at https://lccn.loc.gov/2016014332

Dedicated to those we lost building the punk future

Jeff J. Gresenz

Chris Gaffney

Paul Kissick

Chris Furney

Erika Grove / Erika "Crumbly" Hynes

Ted Cahill

Special thanks to Amy Byrne, Steve Frevert, Barb Orr, Jason Young, Jon Weber, Christina L., Tim Lemke, Tom Williams, Kurt Niesman, Keelan McMorrow, Erv Karwelis, Scott Steele, Mike Rhodes, Jeff Weeter, Brad Towell, Matt Branch, and other donors for providing photos and graphics. My apologies if I forgot others!

INTRODUCTION

For many people, Rockford, Illinois remains merely a rest stop on a flat toll road stretching from Chicago to Madison, Wisconsin. For others, it is the home of porn queen Ginger Lynn, soaring FM rockers Cheap Trick, and the fast food joint Beef-A-Roo. As a product of its northern rim, where the tract homes melded into former farmland owned by stoic Scottish pioneers that founded my parent's church, I know it has also spawned a history of locals going against the grain, including a bevy of young people trying to fulfill the promise of punk to build an underground, do-it-yourself community. What we stirred did not become ingrained in the national underground lore revealed in books like *American Hardcore*. I suppose we were the lesser sons and daughters hatching punk plots, for what we did was in secret, off the grid; an outlier. Fellow punks in Chicago likely scoffed at us as backwater poseurs. Luckily, our struggle— the ups and downs of alienation in the heartland—was not bracketed and tainted by such smugness. Our battle for nonconformity did not make headlines like the metropolis

Rockford, 2014

Rockford, 1992

next door, in which the press examined 'les miserables', the miserable ones in their midst. In New York and Los Angeles, press reports actually inflated the punk scenes by drawing in thousands of kids attuned to headlines that stressed the chaos and violence. In places like Rockford, as denizens of the punk night, our demolition work—attempts to bulldoze stodgy rules, regulations, stereotypes, values—mostly went untold.

Writing about this city is like peeling back a second skin. On the surface of the city in the 1980s, one might see family-time vistas of overflowing churches, bake sales galore, and energetic youth sports leagues. During the anxious years of World War II, the city housed the Peaches, part of the All American Girls Professional Baseball League made famous by the film *A League of Their Own*. Nelson Knitting became famous for designing red-heeled footwear intrinsic to sock monkeys. And in 1949, none other than *LIFE* magazine published a twelve-page spread by a University of Chicago sociologist, titled "A sociologist looks at an American community," which depicted various working classes as a community wrought with bowling nights and kids flocking to ice rinks. Yet, beneath that cosmetic sheen, most of it enabled by local machine tool manufacturers, existed a mess-heap of history ready to implode—a place of inequality, dissent, rancor, and frustration—which rose to the surface as the Cold War began to wind down, foreign competition for contracts kicked into high gear, and long-term salaried jobs began drying up. Rockford was not just another bummed out Midwest town; it became one of the worst, replete with a withering economy and a moral austerity as well. Asking for help was no more than panhandling; one was supposed to be stoic, pull your life up by the bootstraps, even if those straps were haplessly frayed. People's fates often felt jinxed.

So, some eagerly glommed onto punk's sense of caustic rebellion with a cause. They wanted to reshape and retool their lives, if only for the duration of a song in which they could screech until their throats were scorched.

By the 1980s, the weed-invaded Sunset Drive-In theater, with its paint-flaked, baby blue concession stand, flickered with porn films like *Beverly Hills Exposed* in the dark night as kids lurked nearby trying to catch a glimpse. The fecund tree canopy had been ravaged by Dutch Elm Disease in the 1960s (and would be again by Emerald Ash Borer disease in the 2000s). The buildings that lined the train line were mired in broken stonework and graffiti, many company-sponsored sports leagues collapsed, and the skating rinks, VFW, and social halls were about to be rented by punks. A school desegregation lawsuit led white families to yank children from urban schools and flock to the suburbs; meanwhile, unemployment reached 26 percent as the nearby Chrysler plant hemorrhaged jobs. Whereas our parents climbed some version of a ladder of success, my generation felt pinched. We felt the bleakness of go-nowhere minimum wage work, dispiriting factory shift routines, calls to join the military during a ramped-up interventionist period (off to Lebanon, off to Grenada, off to Panama!), and the brain drain of a city whose smartest, art-inclined people often chose to flee.

In 1993, *Money* magazine categorized the town as the worst large city to live in and by the 2000s, Rockford made the national top ten list of cities with the most foreclosures. Punk rock became a soundtrack to

Stu Patterson, 1992

Rockford, 2014

a place fraught with people and places that evoke both a triumphal spirit— people rising above the discord and creating a music, art, and skate scene that survives—and a scary ugliness, including the gritty reality of a city experiencing increasing violence and the aftermath of rust belt industry disintegration. Once thriving factories are mere specters and neglected hulls, perfect for people fetishizing urban decay in YouTube videos. In early 2010, the *Rockford Register Star* declared that heroin use constituted a full-blown, undeniable epidemic. As of 2013, 22 percent of children lived in poverty in the troubled city, 47 percent of African-Americans overall, and the city surged into fourth place in national obesity rankings. And the *Rockford Labor News*, which had published continuously since 1912 in an ongoing

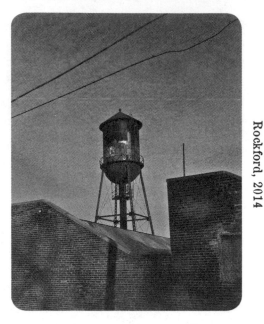

Rockford, 2014

effort to advocate a worker-minded point of view, and also featured street beat reports about the city's law and order conundrums, shut its door for good.

Yet, for over 30 years, a smorgasbord of rulebreakers and dissenters has remained determined and resilient to break out from the doldrums, confusion, despair, and dead city vibes. Like the International Workers of the World (IWW), and radical immigrants who wanted to create a new society within the shell of the old, punks wanted to foster and foment spaces of their own—a sub-city of hope, creation, hard work, spirit, and a version of success, one gig, fanzine, and skatepark at a time.

This is our story.

One

IN THIS PLACE WE CALL HOME

From the late 1800s to early 1900s, the rust belt city blossomed with Scandinavian furniture factories galore, many of them operating as worker collectives, and became ground zero in the Rockford/Wisconsin stateline area for lefties like the IWW, who feverishly fused music and radicalism. In Chicago during Nov. 1915, the union's Rockford branch band, 40 members strong and carrying a defiant red flag, played the funeral of agitator and activist Joe Hill. Wearing ribbons and pennants declaiming, "Don't Mourn—Organize," the mourners, including sturdy working Swedes from Rockford, thronged the streets and drew bemused stares from neighborhood onlookers.

The Swedes in Rockford organized a socialist club as early as 1906 and ran a socialist newspaper in town called the *Svenska Socialisten* (the Swedish Socialist), which bucked the tendency of Swedish townsfolk to vote Republican, and sought to "defend the cause of labor" and "unmask" and hasten the downfall of capitalism, as publisher A. A. Patterson avowed in the premier issue. Local Rockford IWW members, apparently linked to the Furniture Workers and local construction industry, became embroiled in "The Rockford Frame-Up" after they marched in a parade supporting jailed IWW member Clyde Hough and others who refused to sign up for the draft during World War I. Some historians depict the march as 200 surging Finnish immigrants, led by local IWW leader James Cully. Among the Finnish throng were socialists, unionists, and pacifists who opposed the draft due to the U.S. alliance with Russia, their home country's declared enemy. After destroying the plumbing and windows of the city jail, the mob was corralled into nearby small town jails. Under pressure from the U.S. Justice Department, the stern judge sentenced over a hundred of these "Rockford Rebels" to hard labor. Fearing locals would free the men, they were sent by sealed railroad car to the Chicago House of Correction.

Next, during the paranoia catalyzed in 1920, more than 150 citizens, among them many 'alien' Swedes, were nabbed in so-called Palmer raids, the anti-immigrant/anti-communist raids ordered by the Attorney General, often for no more than singing "red" songs at meetings, refusing the draft, and befriending leftists. Of the group, 58 were shipped back to their home countries. The authorities tried to make the city safe for unfettered free market capitalism in the post-war era of rapid industrial growth. Though not all punks shared that Northern European DNA, or were as drawn to the left-wing causes as much as me, we were all products of a boom-to-bust economy that soared, then soured and sputtered. Some parents of these wayward, intransigent kids who crudely shaved their pale heads, donned scuffed combat boots, ripped their jeans to shreds, and grabbed ratty guitars and duct-taped drum sets, were unionist agitators.

By the 1980s, Rockford was a patchwork of rusting factories, hospitals competing for the dead and dying, rivers overflowing like spilled soup, Tee-ball games in front of the psychiatric hospital, feral kids free-diving into reservoirs filled with sunken cars, and a downtown queer-friendly art café that provided a lifeline to progressives, punks, and outsiders. The city felt like dead-end America, the last gasp of a diminished industrial era, a neglected microcosm of simmering woe masked by suburban sprawl: endless fast-food chains lining major streets, and the clean neon of malls, clinics, fast food, and insurance agencies

replaced the corn stubble, dilapidated Victorian homes, and leftover prairie. Despite our parents' best intentions, despite the promise of brand new toys, tall spires of Christmas trees, coiffured green lawns, and fireworks abuzz at holidays, the suburbs were just as vexed and poisoned as the blighted avenues surrounded by crumbling homes in the wards. I vividly recall the guy who shot gas station clerks, the kid who beat and burned a high school counselor, and the stoner metalhead with an X-men comic fixation that tied me to a pole and rubbed Kleenex full of mayonnaise in my face. These were not rare moments. These were everyday experiences among my neighbors. One held his family hostage with a hunting rifle, another got his fingers chopped off in a clamorous factory, and another gassed himself to death in a lonely garage in a ranch home identical to the rest of ours.

A handful of kids like me turned to Dead Kennedys, Agent Orange, and Black Flag because their songs told our truths: we didn't live in candy-coated histories, in safe zones, in a Nick at Night sitcom. In contrast to such Teflon-coated glee and sentimentality, we found a roach wiggling in Chinese food on 7th street, knew kids who traded stolen scratched CDs to buy booze, watched slasher flicks as pot smoke swirled thick as molasses, and looked for sex in all the wrong places. Many of us were touched by creeps or merely forgotten and ignored by dispirited families. We devoured singles by TSOL and DOA, melted toy soldiers with WD40, shot golfballs at neighbors' homes, and built homemade skate ramps so severely verted that we should have broken our bones but instead kept our scrawny bodies afloat on the soundwaves of Italian hardcore pioneers Raw Power and DC's all-Black Bad Brains.

I grew up in ranch home infested Machesney Park, where teenagers blared AC/DC from windows, stomped around in flea-ridden basements, swallowed Coke for breakfast, fingered Nintendo incessantly, and crashed motorcycles into stop signs as yellow spiders roamed corn fields. I patched together a makeshift drum set including a busted snare and a plastic bin from the potato chip factory, then learned "1969" by the Stooges. My room incubated punk gig flyers, a waterbed that leaked, books by Gide, Genet, Camus, and beatniks, and VHS tapes from music fanzine *Flipside* and skate company *Thrasher*. My sister cranked out 999, David Bowie, Gun Club, and Paul Revere and the Raiders from her glaring pink room. My brother brought home dog-eared copies of Siouxsie and the Banshees, Cockney Rejects, and PiL.

My first band was Vital Signs, a super-lean three-piece with no bass. As "Dave Vital" (and later, "Diehard Dave"), my scribbled lyrics (like "Straight and Alert!") poorly mimicked straightedge progenitors Minor Threat and Uniform Choice. I was immediately drawn to the anti-drugs, anti-drinking, anti-meaningless sex messages of straight-edge, which I considered a defiance against punk's drug-drenched debauchery. In fifth grade, I sold stolen weed to other students, experienced molestation, and witnessed rampant beer, heroin, acid, speed, and opium use ravage families. So I fell hard for the adrenalin-induced speed, non-negotiable commitment to all-ages spaces and family-like camaraderie, and the heart-punching choleric wall-of-sound of bands on Dischord, BYO, Touch and Go, Wishingwell, and other record labels that demonstrated similar values. More than a buzzword, it gained traction with kids like me, but others demonized it as no more than an annoying, cellophane-thin, and sham gospel of affirmation that seemed more about boosting T-shirt sales than countering the crude punk mythology of despair, debauchery, dismay, and discord. When positive punk translated into "hardline" or the machismo of bands like Bold and Gorilla Biscuits, I leaned towards Soul Side, whose angular rhythms were powered by funk-punk (even global beat), and whose political nuance seemed more attuned to a struggle for justice than a series of gruff pleas for bodily health, mental fortitude, and vegetarian diets. Soul Side's style evolved into a template for bands like Rage Against the Machine and Propagandhi. As my own band prepped for a stripped-down three-song demo, my mom calmly read in a sofa chair with sheer Methodist determination and patience upstairs. I knew music mattered. It became my orbit.

After dropping out of college in 1990, I married a fellow punk and moved downtown near the Democratic headquarters and regal City Hall. On the second floor of our 1873 building, I stared from my gritty-orange couch through smudged windows to see bellowing, flannel-wearing workmen, and watch drunks jump angrily from the bar next door and threaten tow truck drivers. Across the hall, an amateur bodybuilding champion bulked up on a steady diet of chicken and rice, while a few doors down an old woman smoked cigarettes endlessly and knocked on my door one night with a collapsed lung.

For five years I worked at Appletree Records, a small chain store that served as an alternative to the soulless Musiclands that dotted nearby malls. Appletree stirred a local punk ecology—bands dropped off demos to be strewn across their shelves. I bought innumerable treasures there—cheap Italian import cut-out Dead Kennedys vinyl, the last LP by the Big Boys, 45s by the Minutemen. Our revolving door of customers were doctors, pre-teens making DIY cassettes, security alarm installers, computer techs, factory third shifters, deadheads trying to barter and steal, pizza boys, grocery clerks, and Bun E. Carlos of Cheap Trick.

Cheap Trick came out of Rockford as mavericks of sound and style during the dizzying late 1970s. They unleashed indelible, inexhaustible, guitar-savvy hooks, soaring sun-bleached melodies, occasional grind and crunch, as well as crystalline vocals, all anchored by ductile Carlos, a human metronome on drums who looked like a bored Xerox salesman and an early adopter of a hipster moustache. Much has been written about the glue that held together these underdogs trying to survive in a world of excess, and the clueless executives that forced the band to release the hammy tune

"The Flame," which the band did not pen, but outsold all their other music. One thing remains clear, though: Cheap Trick were bona fide students of music history. They mastered a forceful, kinetic blend of vintage Brit pop, all-American high school swagger, and homegrown garage rock'n'roll.

Unlike most bands on the FM dial, they retained street cred; the band remained resilient and evoked humor and a wonky sense of playfulness symbolized by the outlandish gouache sweaters and facial gymnastics of guitarist Rick Nielsen. They embodied the work ethic of their not-so-distant immigrant ancestors who were eager to rise above.

The career of Nielsen started with 1960s stints in bands such as the Phaetons and the Boyz. He joined bassist Tom Peterson (later, Tom Petersson) first in the Grim Reapers in 1967 and the Fuse in 1968. By early 1970, Epic Records released their self-titled album stateside and in Holland, including tunes like "Mystery Ship" and "Across the Skies." Yet, Nielsen (known for his Midwest bluntness) felt the album was a sub-par affair marred by the producer's poor instincts and abilities. Soon, he planted himself in Philadelphia and re-formed the Fuse with Petersson under the name Sick Man of Europe, whose line-up featured soon-to-be-legend Brad Carlson/Bun E. Carlos on drums. After a short stint, though, they fled the city and returned to the rust belt. The trio became the nexus of Cheap Trick.

Joined by Robin Zander's richly-hued, woven-by-honey vocals that could also be blistering and biting, the band's sensibilities became nuanced and extensive. They loved ELO, Bob Dylan (covering "Lovin' Money"), Velvet Underground (covering "Waiting for the Man/Heroin") the Beatles (Nielsen and Carlos played on the Lennon sessions for *Double Fantasy*), and many more icons. Eventually, the band jumped from playing a regional gig circuit of bars in nearby college and manufacturing towns to a deal with CBS Records, including albums tweaked by producers like Tom Werman, George Martin, and Todd Rungren.

They opened for KISS and The Kinks; meanwhile, on other fabled gigs, like the Winnebago County Fair, AC/DC *opened for them.* They released the smash double-LP *Live at Budokon,* which launched an arena rock career. As the aerosol-stimulated big hair rock ballads of the mid-1980s blurred into the 1990s, the band became keenly interested in the emergent "alt rock" scene, especially the hard hooks and proto-primitive rock'n'roll of "grunge."

While all the members were visible and nonchalant shoppers throughout Rockford at local galleries and events, Bun E. Carlos would stop at outlets like Appletree Records, extol bands like the Dave Clark Five, run his fingers through LP stacks (then the cellophane rows of boxed CDs), hungry to find new voices and unreleased or re-released items, culled from the back catalog of bands entering the digital age. I made him a mixtape from my own vinyl stash, a soundtrack to the age in transition, featuring super-charged, fuzz-laden bands like Mudhoney and Sonic Youth. Not long after, as I sat in Metro Centre impatiently waiting for them with thousands of other locals, they played Sonic Youth's *Goo* over the PA. I smiled, knowing this was inspired by my mixtape. Cheap Trick made a huge impression on the punk generation, inspiring singers like Tony Cadena of the Adolescents and John Brannon of Negative Approach: in turn, punk bands from the pop punk powerhouse Big Drill Car to the noisy Steel Pole Bathtub covered Cheap Trick songs. Cheap Trick were soldiers of pop who merged good looks with geekdom, like misfits in a world of soda pop commercials and dying record labels trying to sell one more Elton John CD-single. Locally, they were jukebox heroes, elders, and stars that didn't seem mired in sordid extravagance and lame clichés.

The always affable and generous Carlos moonlighted in his band the Bun E. Carlos Experience in the early 1990s too, which covered "Motor City is Burning" by the MC5. Ever thankful for my time and suggestions at Appletree, he made me a tape of bootleg MC5 recordings. By the late 1990s, Cheap Trick recorded with the heralded underground label Sub Pop and used studio-svengali Steve Albini, whose noise band Big Black covered "He's a Whore" in 1987. Last time I saw Cheap Trick, Wayne Kramer of the MC5 opened up the show. Knowing Bun E. Carlos saw the MC5 at Forest Hills in Rockford, and recalling the bootleg tape, I knew this was no accident. These were brothers-in-arms of the musical insurrection, and the circle had become complete; after witnessing the trajectories of such men, rust city kids like me knew we could save the day, or make each day an inch more bearable, by unleashing sheer voltage and

Tim Lemke, 1992

savvy tunes to turn the tide of one's history. We didn't have to be stuck in a morass; we could reinvent ourselves, break our molds.

Stuart Patterson, Charles St., 1991

Two

THE ROOTS OF THE REBELLION

Although the late 1980s were awash in gigs featuring coast-to-coast punk bands traveling through Rockford's smalltown night, the real roots for the fecund underground community were sown by a previous generation of rock'n'rollers, outsiders, and misfits. Deep in the history of Rockford existed pre-punk bands like The Jacemen in the 1960s. Their singer, Jim Friis, also fronted garage rockers Valiants, who had an up-tempo tune and clean production, hound dog vocals, and fiery guitar solo. Listening to these tunes today, when much music has become full of programmed beats and Auto-Tuned vocals, they remind me that almost every large town had a version of Chuck Berry, Jerry Lee Lewis, and Little Richard—rockers unfastening a brazen, unfiltered soundtrack to the times when rock'n'roll was recorded live in one-room studios or garages. These early efforts prove that behind the façade of prim and proper society promulgated by the *LIFE* article existed a raving culture in Rockford.

By the 70s and 80s, another Rockford group called the Names had released the single "Why Can't It Be." Meanwhile, locals acts like Davey and The Daggerz, the tough'n'tumble rockabilly act Rocky and the Squirrels, and The Sharp Turn, whose track "Everybody Knows But Me" (which resembles 1960s fuzz rock like the Chocolate Watchband) landed on the notorious *Battle of the Garages Vol. II* (Voxx Records, 1984), seem closer in spirit to the Jacemen. They offered garage rock ruckus in a time when the radio dial was drooling with Olivia Newton-John, Lionel Richie, and Steve Miller Band.

John Sherman experienced that initial wave of Rockford punk firsthand as a founding member of The Sharp Turn. "The Sharp Turn were [originally] called The Detours. I got us the first gig any of us played at the Harlem Park Boys Club Battle of the Bands where we had a movie light-bar with red, green, and blue flood lights on a color organ. I played key-tar poorly on the gym floor. The other band had a full stage with PA, rigging, and light show. We made long-time friends there [though] we weren't all old enough to drive. I stopped trying to add a monophonic synth to a Mod band and became the soundman. We changed the name to The Uranium Frames, some other names, then The Sharp Turn. They were my friends from Auburn [High School], which had an active magnet-school program and a low power radio station." Like many in the scene, such bands gestated their sound by trial and error, often in the public eye during 'showcases' that set one band against another in pursuit of small-time glory. The local schools, at one time equipped with ample music programs and even radio opportunities, also became a breeding ground for experimenting. Students could test their interests and give some free reign to their interests outside the mandated, lifeless textbook curriculum.

The Sharp Turn soon journeyed into the regional network, including stints across the border into Wisconsin, into college territories like Northern Illinois University and Illinois State University, or to

Chicago, where they felt welcomed. Sherman tweaked the soundboard at one gig, learning to hone his skills and learn the physical routines of rock'n'roll. "I recorded with one channel off the board and the other with a boundary mic," he recalls. "Matt Allison was playing guitar with them and did the token guitar-smashing thing. That band was a big part of my window into the world back then. One of the singers that Detours/Frames/Turn auditioned was Paul Kissick." The band explained there was, "This guy who hangs around with punks, but he's a big fan of [pop songsmith] Todd Rundgren."

With dramatic singer/guitarist Kissick at the helm, PineWood Box set the stage for my immersion in live local music. They had some roots in North Park where "normal" teens worshipped local teen metal bands and sleaze rockers. The blue collar stretch of road featured a Chinese restaurant where I always ordered a burger, an Army Navy surplus store crowded with dingy combat boots, Logli's grocery store, a comic book store that offered paperbacks by J.G. Ballard, a thrift store yielding *Sandinista* by the Clash and 1960s slacks, and a no-frills soft serve ice cream stand. Their own slanted soundtrack of the times evolved repeatedly; at first rooted in surf punk nerviness, it eventually tapped industrial music's insistent metallic anti-dance grind. By the late 1980s, if you paid to see a PineWood Box gig, a shuddering sonic maelstrom combined with a cryptic Darkwave environment immersed you.

Kissick led previous bands Zero-Types and Near Mrs., as well as Juicy Fiance, with Johnson. Juicy Fiance released one cassette that endures. "I still have it," Stu Patterson insists, "and listen to it once in a while. Paul sang in a very cool fake British accent, and Dwight Anderson played ripping saxophone riffs over everything." Kissick exuded flair with ease and became a legend simply by forgoing defeatism and wanky rock clichés. "Paul wrote in such a way that the meaning changed every time he sang a verse. Within the same song, he'd change gender, emotion or even flip the whole context of the song," tells "Scary" Dan Gildea, who built sets for the band.

Early on, PineWood Box mixed Southern California-slanted surf punk with early trembling Cure and guitar shattering 1970s Dead Boys and Johnny Thunders on tunes like "I Can't Change" and "Running from Yourself." Later choice cuts like "Obsession" channeled Bauhaus, "Shadows" does not seem far removed from 45 Grave, "100 Days" lifts some ambience from Sisters of Mercy, and agitated "Skate" tells the story of skateboard death-trip Tommy by revealing a Cramps-like rockabilly romp. By the mid-1980s, punk had long been overtaken by the rigid formulas of hardcore; often, the genre felt regimented and orthodox, because it offered a lot of sheer speed and fury without a whole lot of experimentation. PineWood Box preserved the original premises of punk; just like the heady, fluid years of 1974-1978, they emulated bands that pulled from a variety of sources, mixed and matched styles, and defied genre boundaries

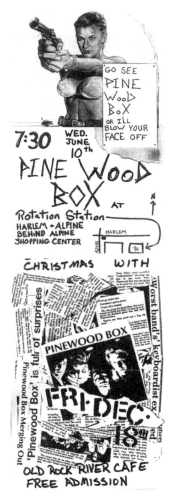

and definitions. They seemed to change their music whenever the mood, impetus, or desire felt right. This was the true template of the Clash, Buzzcocks, Wire, Siouxsie and the Banshees, and more. One of Box's tunes, "Life's a Beach," was inserted on the compilation *Oversea Connection*, released by German company Double A Records in 1987; this gave other local bands a sense of hope and pride—they too could appeal to a global audience.

One aspect that always felt alive and well in terms of the band's modus operandi was their campy ongoing dedication to spookiness and monster movie aesthetics. Their flyers were awash in images of women in bras bearing enormous pistols, acting as a rogue female Dirty Harry, or menacing ghouls in top hats. They were not alone in these ventures. Regionally, bands in Michigan like Zombie Surfers as well as 3-D Invisibles picked up a similar mantle; their flyers appropriated Rat Fink, comic book, and vintage film images. Nationally the Misfits adopted a similar aesthetic: oiled wisps of devilock hair, warlock ambience, sexual fetish gear, and white-painted faces.

"Kissick recruited me to help him put together cool horror stage shows. He thought I could help him because I went to art school, was a sculptor, and I am a big haunted house enthusiast and had worked on numerous haunted house events," tells Gildea. "The band was just Paul, Nick Thomas, and Dan Whyte, who left early on. I asked my friend Randy Rainwater, another big haunted house enthusiast, to play drums. A short while later, Paul asked me to play an old broken-down organ during practices." Like a plethora of punk's founders, faulty instruments and a lack of skills added authenticity to punk's ethos. Intention and raw desire meant much more than careful plans and by-the-book precepts.

PineWood fulfilled those precedents. "I didn't play any instruments, but Nick helped me figure out what keys to play. I eventually learned some simple chords so I could play music beds behind the band, but mostly I was responsible for a lot of noise and sound effects." But those sound effects added dense layers that made the band seem otherworldy at times. "Later on, I used tape loops and other devices to 'enhance' the sound ... That lineup became the first visible iteration of PineWood Box."

Randy Rainwater created art and props. Meanwhile, Jeff Lierman, Dwight Gail (R.I.P.) and Trace Evans managed staging and special effects. Stan Musialek (R.I.P.) made masks and props, while Rick Ruiz (R.I.P.) did staging and rigged lighting. With no budget, these people, alongside others, created theatrical Ed Wood B-movie-style shows straight out of old Hollywood. They shot promotional pics in cemeteries vamping alongside an old hearse, pretending to dig up skulls, and even lying down on graves.

PineWood Box's mystique emanated from their sonic mixology and creative stage shows but also from the tragedy enfolded in the band's losses, including those above plus founding member Paul Kissick and plenty more. "Add Kyle Nieman (R.I.P.), Nick Thomas (R.I.P.), Jason Yeager (R.I.P.), and Tom Nali (R.I.P.) to the memorials," explains Gildea, "and you'll see what seems to be an incredibly high death toll associated with PineWood Box. These people died in a variety of ways. Some through accidents or violence, others succumbed to illness or chose to opt out on their own."

Kissick was brutally killed at age 39, another Rockford rocker ravaged, lost to time. His prescient lyrics, though, remain clearly etched:

"This city has closed my eyes and it's pain for me to take/

If I can't deal with it, what's the sense of going on and on

I'm going to another place, somewhere, I don't care, away/

When I get there I'll be anything I want to"

In response to allegations of a PineWood Box "curse," Gildea stresses, "If we wait long enough, everyone who ever played in, associated with, or went to see PineWood Box will die. That's the curse."

Another colorful character whose stature looms large is Louie Name: "Louie and Don Bush had a punk/beer/Nazi-flag-outside-the-window/dumpster-couch kinda place in 1980 or '81," notes John Sherman. "I hung out with them before I knew they actually played. Later, Allan and I saw Louie at The Escape in a band called Studs Terkel. Lou wore an American flag and crowd-surfed while playing guitar until the crowd tried to take the guitar!" Louis, who played a Flying V guitar for the Near Mrs. seemed to be the local avatar of all things punk and roamed the city streets as the old guard of local bedlam boys. "Louie, Don, and Mary Valuis were all people who were just punk by nature," Patterson recalls. "It wasn't really a choice they made. They were just misfits/rebels. Louie rode around town on a moped sporting a Mohawk. I witnessed him shoot himself with a taser gun one night and decided

Soul Side and Swiz at
Rotation Station, 1988

that we would not be friends any time soon!" Though this may seem bizarre in the post-hardcore punk era, such anything-goes Dionysian exploits were normal behavior in the early 1980s.

The first club gig I saw was uber-power pop unit the Flex, which Sherman anchored on bass at the time, at a bar near Northern Illinois University. I had not reached age sixteen yet, so when my sister's boyfriend offered to take me along, I jumped in his tiny red car and we cranked home-taped albums by X on the way. For years, I experienced punk vicariously—basking in my brother's stories of seeing the Cramps and Black Flag, for instance, watching VHS tapes or absorbing the live appearances of bands like the Clash on *Saturday Night Live*. Seeing the Flex on the dim-lit stage with a handful of people undulating to the tightly-coiled beat set forth my plans. I needed to re-make my life, enter the brave new world, and grow up as soon as possible. Soon, I was planning my own gigs, even if that meant playing my own basement to friends you could count on one hand; using cut, paste, and press-on letter techniques to forge a Xeroxed fanzine, and scribbling letters back and forth across swaths of the pre-Internet country.

Sherman's band Duck and Cover (also variously known as Toy Division, etc.) included wiry guitarist John Hessian, who described their project as a "fun ... punk band" in the debut issue of *No Deposit No Return*, my zine named after a Henry Rollins spoken word track from *Family Man*, which I kicked into gear in 1987. "If the Replacements can put out an album called *Let it Be*," Hessian joked in the interview, "we're going to put out one called *Houses of the Holy*. We'll have a picture of us stoned on a roof, just kidding." This early interview gave me the courage to leapfrog to regional acts like Life Sentence and Defoliants, and national and international acts within a year or two.

Neo-punk bands from the era include The Iks who grew out of a rockabilly outfit called The Buicks. At the time, given the popularity of acts like Stray Cats and The Meteors, whose styles were a full-blown return to the hiccupy, swinging, feral rock'n'roll style of the 1950s, this was not uncommon. But with songs like "My Dad's Ganglion," "I'm Not Black," and "Cranium Assault," the Iks embodied a converging, mutating sense of genres in which world-class musicians played a "punk-meets-funk, late-period Clash meets B-52's kind of mix that was way beyond anything going on in Rockford at the time," recalls Stu Patterson. "Their record reminds me of the Minutemen when I listen to it now, and their live shows were always a funky dance party. They were together for three or four years, played in Chicago mostly, and broke up after one of them was injured in a bike accident." The sober ballad, "City at Three," howled in a husky timber, explores the underground that thrives due to insomnia ("I'm alive while you're asleep!"). "Too Butch" waxes ironically about a lesbian lover that topples gender codes by not cooking and making the male narrator feel he's the one likely to get pregnant, while "We're Trying" skewers middle-class America: "A chicken in every pot / two cars in every garage / In each room of TV—that's all you can see." The closest they game to full-throttle punk is the choppy, aggressive "War." Their legacy remains intact because they set a high bar; many people I interviewed for this book insisted, "Don't forget the Iks, man." Their effective mishmash style, recording contract, and caliber of playing meant that future bands didn't have to repeat the same stunted chords of a million garage bands. They were local antecedents, local heroes, that helped pave a fecund and imaginative path.

SNFU, 1988

Three
WHERE THE WILD ONES THRIVE

Hardcore became a variant of punk even more brutally shorn of excess, more direct and pummeling, more hammering and truculent. Antecedents surely existed in the first wave of punk, like Wire, whose situationist political stances and short, sharp tunes like 1977's "12XU" were avidly covered by a few hardcore progenitors. The prototypes of this new rank and file style were: the Middle Class' "Out of Vogue" (1979) single, which amounts to a speed-emblazoned, frenzied, stripped-down assault, plus albums by the Los Angeles punk pioneers Germs (*GI*, 1979), New York's Plasmatics (*New Hope for the Wretched*, 1980) led by the charred, gnarly voice of Wendy O. Williams, and the Bad Brains "Pay to Cum" (1980) single, as well as the EP *In God We Trust, Inc.* (1981) by the Dead Kennedys, which gave up none of the seismic snarl or snarky dark humor of their first album *Fresh Fruit for Rotting Vegetables*. These recordings greatly impacted both American and European punk communities, but felt much more cut-throat and minimal—the unadorned music harnessed a bulldozing kind of bluntness, manic propulsion, and nitrous-injected energy.

Jeremy Kunz, 1988

Polygenesis occured, though: bands dotting the musical landscape, which was in upheaval, also formulated their own similar, broiling responses to punk— Discharge, DOA, Void, the Faith, MDC, Offenders, Dicks, Black Flag, and manifold others developed their unique trademarks and stamps of defiance. But much of that seemed relegated to larger cities, where college radio, hip record shops, and alternative film centers held sway. Early on, smaller heartland towns outside the college belts often lacked the sheer resources needed to

sustain ongoing communities. So, the hardcore genre hiccupped into Rockford a few years later than it did in Chicago, where Articles of Faith exercised impressive flashes of limber musicality as early as 1981. In Rockford, the scene fostered a quick uprising due to a handful of diligent, sometimes delinquent youth, and a persistent crop of bands dedicated to experimenting with style, content, and vision.

The younger generation did not have the same set of idols in their sites; whereas the older set loved the soundtrack of the Blank Generation, the name given to the era that spawned controversial, subversive, and witty rock'n'roll titans like the Sex Pistols, Dead Boys, and Fear. The post-1984 generation looked to the new breed that gestated under Ronald Reagan's first term, which was often geared to an all ages crowd—Corrosion of Conformity, Suicidal Tendencies, DRI, Minor Threat, 7 Seconds, Gang Green, MDC, and more. These were the bands lauded by *Maximum Rocknroll*, the monthly bible for the hardcore

Tad Keyes, Kinkos, 1992

generation, yet many of the bands soon developed cross-over urges: they merged the stylized, dueling, controlled, rhythmic riffage of speed metal (Venom, Motorhead) with dirtier, wrenching thrash (Megadeath, Slayer). Sure, some crossover existed between generations, but the kids who began setting up a new network in Rockford aimed to rejuvenate it—to take music from the bars to skating rinks, rented halls, and all ages clubs. This meant crowds became more inclusive, democratic, and youthful, less geared to booze-fueled tirades and more fueled by slam dancing and skate-till-death/skate-and-destroy mentalities. Soon, gigs were attracting hundreds of kids zooming in from miles in every direction. The punk nucleus widened considerably. The 'burbs poured in. And the older generation felt less inclined to join us. Some of them preferred the up'n'coming school of pre-grunge (Green River) and post-hardcore/noise/acid-punk rock stirring the scene (Laughing Hyenas, Scratch Acid, Butthole Surfers), or were content to follow their own early 1980s punk heroes like Hüsker Dü, Replacements, and Soul Asylum, who all signed to major labels and "matured" their sound.

Situated halfway between Madison and Chicago, as the DIY touring network cohered in the mid-1980s, Rockford became a depot for bands crisscrossing the flatlands. Just as important, working-class and middle-class kids with supportive parents—both psychologically and financially—became the backbone of a portion of the scene. These crews could build stages, rent halls and PAs, buy sodas for resale, and provide space for bands to sleep and eat. In the beginning, Old Rock River Café and Deli downtown featured the likes of Soul Asylum; meanwhile, Bloodsport, Blatant Dissent, Naked Raygun, and Black Flag gigged at the Channel. Greg Ginn twisted like a Tourette's patient stitched to his guitar, roiling on stage in a repetitive blur as Henry Rollins acted hammy. Cantankerous locals hooted "Gimme Gimme Gimmee" in the dank room, while I stood too close to the sizzling, stacked PA. Outside, as we poured onto the sidewalks, a dozen or so cops kept careful watch, even blurted "Boy, keep moving" as I crept by them, head slightly drooped. If they were expecting an L.A. riot to fester on the spot, instead they met kids straggling by, ready for late-night runs to Burger King.

Another wave of involvement began to crest. The hardcore scene kicked into high gear, especially due to Tad Keyes' arrival from Madison, WI. He helped organize shows at the Polish Falcon's Club, a VFW hall, and an old grocery store for SNFU, NOFX, Dag Nasty, Fugazi, Scream, and Uniform Choice. I met Keyes at a basement show featuring Operation Ivy. After checking out the fanzine that my dad printed after hours at his factory for me, Keyes strode up, smiling. We both embodied a close-to- the-heart sincerity partly inspired by Better Youth Organization, an organization focused on shaping punk into a positive social impact. The loose-knit organization, which sprang up in a few locales across the country, was mostly the offspring of Shawn Stern, the singer and guitarist of Youth Brigade in Los Angeles.

During the mid-1970s, Shawn and his brothers had been skateboaders, surfers, and multi-instrumentalists (Shawn could also play saxophone) who first heard punk on the radio— "My Aim is True" by Elvis Costello—and then dove into the scene firsthand by forming the new-wavy Extremes, who gigged with the likes of the Bags, Zeros, and Go-Go's. They

transitioned Youth Brigade by cross-pollinating doo-wop, Shakespeare, and early rap with hardcore 'sound and fury' (the actual title of their first album as well). The brothers were entrepreneur types who dispensed candy in high school, sold drugs, and put on keg parties. But after converting to the punk-cum-hardcore ethos, the Stern brothers briefly rented a house they nicknamed Skinhead Manor, a place for kids to flop, booked tumultuous shows at places like Godzillas and the Olympic, which helped catalyze a Los Angeles scene numbering in the thousands, jumpstarted their record label BYO (which housed SNFU, 7 Seconds, Bouncing Souls, and Leatherface), and penned hopeful songs like "Fight to Unite" and "Something to Believe In." Their ethos seemed simple: project a side of punk that wasn't merely wanton and debauched. Like the IWW, they sought to build something new within the shell of the old. Avoid the contradictions of the bureaucratic systems that selectively hold people back and repress talent and urges: the record industry (go DIY, bypass them!), the media monopolies (become the media: make your own fanzine, pirate radio show, or flyer!), and the family-civil authority nexus (create your own family-like communities and networks of trust). Remake business as usual. Locally, Tad Keyes and his coterie helped me pursue those same goals in Rockford.

"When I became aware of punk music as a kid in 1980 it was a stylized version of what had started in America, gone over to England, and come back as new wave and power pop," recalls Keyes. "While bands like Devo and Blondie were on the radio, even those popular high-style versions of punk felt dangerous. It was a fascinating, weird, new movement that adults did not like. By the time punk finally hooked me completely, it had changed again, informed by post punk and Oi. It was once again American, and we were calling it hardcore. It was faster and more pragmatic and had lost some of the original 'weird for weirdness' sake' ethos. This was the punk that spoke to suburban and working class teens across the U.S."

author at WBCR, Beloit, 1989

For kids like Keyes, "going punk" in 1984 meant making a statement. "It meant choosing sides. It stirred up controversy, invited violence, and tested friendships and family bonds," he attests. "Punk was like a personal protest rally that brought out the bad cop in teachers, parents, and schoolyard alphas." It incited reaction, often in the most reactionary of forms, by friends and family, or those who hated anyone questioning routines and habits. "Punk was the earliest and most adolescent version of politics I had access to. Even if the conflict created was largely contrarian in nature and more style than substance—it was still good practice." And practice, or what may be termed praxis, is what Keyes would excel at. But first, he underwent punk's rites of passage.

The year Ronald Reagan's campaign for re-election steamrolled across the states, Keyes began his deep immersion. "Questioning authority was in vogue; everyone from Jello Biafra to my 8ᵗʰ grade English teacher had something to say about Orwell's *1984*. In the first four years of Reagan's rule, American hardcore had grown outspokenly political, and 90 percent of punks were on the left, if only because Reagan was on the right. There was a 'my enemy's enemies are my friends' effect going on; Reagan supported the Contras, we rooted for the Sandinistas. Reagan and Thatcher busted unions, so the unions became folk heroes."

"The state of the second wave of American punk, or hardcore, was also weird," Keyes acknowledges too. Though much more youth-friendly than pioneering punk, hardcore's zenith, circa 1982, had peaked, "and the bands that had built the hardcore movement were breaking up or changing styles almost monthly," he recalls. By the mid-1980s, DRI, Corrosion of Conformity, Suicidal Tendencies, and Gang Green leaned towards metal riffage and song patterns. "We had just missed Minor Threat and the Misfits; instead, we got Black Flag and DOA with long hair and long songs." Hüsker Dü, the Minutemen, the Bad Brains, and Dead Kennedys were still strong, but they too began a mutation phase, yet their early vinyl did inspire "our DIY aesthetic and lifestyle. The real absence was older punks, though. No one over sixteen seemed to care about punk—and definitely no veterans considered it a

Insight in North Park, 1988

life-changing style or even a lifestyle. The few people still booking shows in the mid-80s were the diehards." That's how Keyes became conscious of the gaps he could fill. As the hardcore genre shifted style, new bands emerged, and dependable DIY networks solidified, people like Keyes could harness the moment at hand.

author, 1992

"Through high school, my whole worldview was still based on how everything related to punk. As I got older, my ideas and emotions became more complex and nuanced, and I discovered that there was a whole scene of punks in Washington D.C. that were growing up without abandoning the youth culture of punk: they grew within it and grew the scene into something more complex and nuanced." After some of those bands—Soul Side, Kingface—stayed with Keyes, he took a trip to Washington D.C. with a few friends, visiting Dischord Records. Keyes witnessed a practice by the seminal hardcore-gone-rock'n'roll band Scream, whose line-up included Dave Grohl, who would go on to play in Nirvana and the Foo Fighters. Yet, Keyes also felt a changing mood, scene politic, and genre re-positioning. "The second half of the '80s saw punk maturing and becoming more focused on the personal rather than political. However, the resulting emotionally focused 'hardcore' began to feel narcissistic, and I quickly grew tired of it."

Keyes sums up the mid-1980s as "the worst time to get into an established culture, but the best time to get into a movement if you hoped to have any effect on that movement." He worked at a roller skating rink called Rotation Station on the outskirts of town with walls painted like Colorado landscapes. It had been converted into a makeshift skateboard park mostly due to Rory, a high school classmate of mine, whose mother operated the rink. For years they usually spun quotidian FM rock as skaters whirred by in their stress-free zone under the track lighting. But as Rory came of age and discovered the Misfits and other crops of hardcore giants, the rink began hosting skateboard nights and touring bands, culminating in blistering performances by East Coasters like Psycho, who arrived with a spray-painted banner, and Flag of Democracy from Philadelphia, with their banshee male-vocal wails and furious 130 MPH tempos. West Coasters arrived too, like the Adolescents, whose punk anthems had been a part of lore for years and epitomized the Los Angeles sound. Above all, for kids like me who lived on the distressed and dispirited extended fingers of the city, such gigs made me feel a part of a national uprising. That space became a high school of sorts: a microcosmic horde of kids from miles in every direction became temporarily housed in their own world where we wore our sense of weirdness, angst, and sexual sin like a badge of honor. Plus, we could skate ramps that hurled us against and up painted walls, past broken ceiling tiles, and through empty air itself above a surface smooth as glass. It existed as a site of risk and reward.

Both of my parents were products of traumatized households—their own young mothers struck down by cancer and suicide—so I believe they hoped to create a different kind of home, one where I could explore youth culture, unlike their own serious, undeterred rush to adulthood and stability in the late 1950s. I made my first flyer for the Adolescents gig by Xeroxing a photo from *Flipside* and scrawling the info in loopy penmanship. Swiz stayed the night in the basement of my house next to the nickel-run jukebox and bumper pool table; and singer Shawn Brown was the first African American to stay over. Only a handful of Black students attended my school, so my sense of multiculturalism was often informed far more by television, magazines, and books than the reality on the ground in the 'burbs surrounded by farm plots. Likely, that was true for many punks living outside metroplex areas. So, when Black punks toured the country's inner nexus of sleepy towns, they helped counter segregation and perhaps even began to jumpstart a kind of multiculturalism in places where exposure was limited. The skate center, with its shop teeming with rentable Thrasher videos featuring gay punk icon Gary Floyd and his band the Dicks, or bisexual/cross-dressing/sexually ambiguous Dave Dictor fronting Millions of Dead Cops, not to mention the Powell Peralta boards they carried, became a school of punk shaping the future for kids like me, to the point that I am now friends with both Floyd and Dictor. Local punk fans Scott Steele and Steve Kammerer masterminded some of the early gigs on-site, including incendiary performances by a range of fierce Midwest acts. "In the summer of 1985, we rented the Mexican Patriots Club on Central," tells Steele, "and Steve lined up the bands: Slam from Sweden and Dehumanizers from Seattle, and a handful from Chicago—Number Nine, Insane War Tomatoes, and Denied Remarks. We sold tickets in advance at Appletree Records and 229 Club. We also took some to a record store in Dekalb and put up flyers. About 75 to 100 people showed up. The Dehumanizers stayed at my apartment, and Slam stayed at Steve's house the first night! My girlfriend was a good sport about empty beer cans and bottles all over the place as well as people sleeping out on the balcony. I somehow slept through the ruckus because I had to work the next day, though I was late. Slam

came back to stay at our apartment because Steve's mother kicked them out of her house and I lived nearby. The next day we spent hanging out skateboarding in the drainage ditch, Tony Jannsen from Slam was a pro skateboarder I believe. We also went to someone's backyard half pipe in Machesney Park. I also remember one of the roadies taping my whole Metallica album collection." This experience helps illustrate the sharing economy of punk; for instance, I traded my last pair of leather sneakers to a member of a touring band for a copy of their first album. Another time I gave a band member a copy of a Big Black album as its seething, irascible industrial-punk seemed too demented for me at the time. These exchanges were based on generosity, curiosity, and sometimes old-fashioned bartering; on a small scale level, such acts kept the spirit of punk untainted by sheer profit motives. Plus, the sharing of homes, goods, and even services fostered a sense of community that linked local efforts to regional, national, even global scenes. Touring bands and hometown bands and fans could occupy an inclusive, democratic space together.

But things didn't always go smoothly. The next gig that Steele

organized with three touring bands drew unwanted attention. He recalls, "As show time approached, tons of people showed up on Central, and the police wanted to see what we were doing. They asked if we had a permit. We found out later that we didn't need one, but they told us we had to stop the show. In a panic, we called Sandy at Rotation, who let us use the place, but not until after the open skate was over. She wanted a dollar for each ticket we sold. We agreed, and about 50 kids followed us. The bands' sets were shortened. Life Sentence pretty much got gas money. The others, maybe 100 bucks paid out of our own pockets. It was still a blast, though. Totally fun."

The 1980s was the heyday of radio—college, independent, and pirate—as well as rampant fanzines and public access television. People like Tim Lemke, who sang and played guitar for Headcleaner, chiseled out space for punk culture. He adopted the on-air name 'Simon Cutler' on the Platteville radio station, WSUP, where he DJ'd the late shift, 10 PM-2 AM, always featuring a 'hardcore half hour' at midnight. "One guy I was friends with at the radio station was really into metal and the virtuoso guitar players of the era, like Steve Vai and Joe Satriani," remembers Lemke. "He came to one of our shows and glared at me while I knocked out some sloppy, dissonant, Greg Ginn-inspired guitar riffs, and then left in disgust. I saw him a couple

VERBAL ASSAULT
FROM: NEWPORT ROAD ISLAND

LIVE AT ROTATION STATION
ROCKFORD, IL

WEDNESDAY, APRIL 13,
ALL AGES

Doors Open at 8:00 pm

MORE SHOWS TO COME:
APRIL 30TH - LIFE SEQUENCE
May 14TH - W.O.T.S.
HERE

For more information call 1-800-398-8771
Ted Nagel

SHOW WILL END EARLY SO YOU CAN GET UP FOR SCHOOL AND
—LEARN—

ONLY $3.00

SKATE NITE

Generation Waste

days later. He seemed pissed off and said, 'It looked like you don't know what you're doing. You have no business being on stage.' He was truly offended that we were able to play a show when our technique wasn't as refined as his heroes' and he didn't want to be friends with me after that. Such is life when you play punk."

"Initially, we practiced in an unused office building at the Platteville Municipal Airport," he continues, "just outside of Platteville. And when we were back in Rockford on the weekends and summer we would practice in my parents' basement in Winnebago. While we had some punk/post-punk influences, we certainly weren't a classic 'punk' band. I think at the time we described ourselves as 'alternative ... a mix of post-punk, cow punk, and just straight up rock.'" Like many hardcore kids across the country trying to reckon with their past, Lemke's musical tastes were not rigid or strict, they were an amalgam: "We also mixed in some covers when we played—which were an odd mix of post-punk and old rock songs from bands like the Descendents, Led Zeppelin, Jimmy Hendrix, Bauhaus, Black Flag, and Black Sabbath. We were both big Minutemen (who avidly covered Creedence Clearwater Revival and Blue Öyster Cult) fans too."

"The first time we played in front of an audience was at Winnebago High School. I had been involved in band, musicals, and chorus when I went to school there. The year after I graduated I got a call from the head of the music program at the school. They were facing some budget cuts and were putting together a talent show to raise money and highlight the talent that had come out of the school. She asked if I would be willing to do a performance. I agreed to do something with my new band, but I don't think she had any idea what I had in mind."

Lemke improvised. "We didn't have a bass player yet, so I reached out to Greg Jansen," the bass player for Armed Vision whom he knew from high school. "We played one of the first songs Clell and I wrote called 'A Place to Go,' ... the classic surf song 'Wipeout' too, I have no idea why, and practiced the first time just an hour or so before the show ... working out the changes in one of the classrooms right before we went on."

"That performance was hilarious," Lemke avows. "Most of the performers that day were doing nice, choral songs or performances on typical high school band instruments. We were one of the later acts. We set up behind the curtain, I cranked up my amp and knocked out a couple power chords. Friends who were in the audience told me half the crowd instantly put their hands up to cover their ears. I almost wiped out during that performance too when I jumped up on my amp, forgetting it was on casters, and it started to roll out from under me."

Clell and Tim eventually found bass player Ryan Bielefeldt, who they jokingly referred to as B flat or the Bassmaster General (inspired by The Descendents' line "bass master general came to me" in their jazzy, beatnik, quirky tune "All-O-Gistics"). Soon, the band was gigging in Platteville and at the Mulberry Bush, a bar in Rockford. "For whatever reason, the owner's wife liked us, and we were invited to play every now and then, even though we never drew much of a crowd there," Lemke admits. "I remember a show there when there were more underagers outside listening from the street than there were patrons inside. I think there was some guy passed out at one of the tables too, which is amazing considering how loud we were. The stage in that place was elevated above the bathrooms at the end of the bar and you had to climb a ladder to get up there. It had disgusting, old shag carpeting on the stage. I remember that Clell would often play his drums barefoot and I decided to go barefoot one night at the Mulberry Bush, until I stepped on a chunk of broken glass that was in that nasty carpet."

The trio scraped money to record *Energy*, a four-song cassette recorded on 8-tracks in engineer Jimmy Johnson's basement, in 1987. "I asked him if he'd be OK with me making up a name for the studio when I printed the tape labels. He told me I could call it whatever I want, and I ended up naming it The Underground Noise Chamber. Once he saw that he called me up and asked if I would mind if he used that name. I agreed. He later dropped the 'underground' part because he thought it was too anti-mainstream and he just called his studio The Noise Chamber," Lemke recalls.

Lemke then began to work at the studio. "I became friends with Jimmy, which introduced me to a lot of the musicians ... This led to us opening for Right Mind, a pretty big pop rock band in Rockford at the time. We were not a good opening act [in front of] preppy white folks. They hated us! Throughout the show, the crowd booed and chanted, 'We want Right Mind!' until I said, 'This is our last song', then they finally cheered us ... the Right Mind guys were really cool, though! They were unhappy with the audience for being a bunch of dicks."

Other confrontational moments occurred as well. "The woman I was dating at the time went to drop fliers for one of our upcoming shows on the windshields of cars in the parking lot," Lemke remembers. "She came across one car where a woman was giving a guy a blowjob, so she took one of our Headcleaner fliers and slapped it on their windshield saying, 'You might need this!'"

One of Headcleaners' most infamous peers was Rockford's acerbic Bludgeoned Nun, who embodied a sense of no-bullshit, working class grit more than any other band on the scene. They seemed like merchants of a very dark, bristling, vociferous anger creeping right out of the moribund shacks that dotted the city's blighted sides. Gary Manning, their imposing singer, was a blend of schizoid animosity and virulent musicality.

"It was 1978-79 when I was a freshman or sophomore in high school and discovered punk," Manning recalls. "I had heard of the Sex Pistols, and since I was kind of an outcast and loved live, raw music, I tried to find anything I could. I would get *Creem*. Back then they would have stories, interviews, and pictures of punks. Anything I could find I wanted. As time went on, I heard the Plasmatics and bought everything I could from Appletree Records. Then I got a hold of *Fresh Fruit for Rotting Vegetables* from the Dead Kennedys. It was fast, abusive, thought-provoking, and took on the machine, which I loved, having grown up with just enough to get by ... I wanted to have a name that pissed you off and a sound and show that made you go shit." Some of the shit was caused merely by the band's name. "Well, with our band name, you can imagine. Getting banned from venues for just a name, or a promoter getting protested for setting up a show, like churches and women organizations, you name it, so it was a challenge, but it was what I loved and still do." Looking back, and even in the midst of the period, people suggest the name is misogynist, that it seems like a cue to maim and kill; in fact, I believe the name is a not-so-secret reference to wars in locales like El Salvador, in which para-militaries routinely executed nuns and priests in the most severe, grotesque ways. Hence, the chilling name acts as a geo-political allusion to Reagan era proxy wars.

ROCKFORD'S ONLY

BLUDGEONED NUN

WITH

THE

F.U.C.T.

CHAINSAW PRODUCTIONS
MIKE SIMMS

MARCH 19TH SAT.
MADISON, WI
THE NEIGHBORHOOD HOUSE
29 SOUTH MILLS
ALL AGES

Dating back to 1984, they carved out music now typically described as grindcore—abrasive, crusty, noise-thronged—unleashed in songs like "Jimmy Swaggart Makes Me Sick" and "Concentration Camp," which depicted President Reagan shredding human rights and placing non-conformers in camps teeming with "mind manipulation in human trance." To be sure, though, they were not politically correct, or a Rockford version of anarcho Profane Existence bands that soon thrived in cities like Minneapolis. They were more malevolent. As the epitome of fierce and frenzied, they fit perfectly on bills with touring bands such as Accused, who shared a zealous sense of crushing speed and a twisted sense of the macabre. The first line-up featured Jeff Kersch on guitar, tells Manning. "We played a little party at Jeff's house, his sister's party. It was a trial run, I guess."

"Our first cassette had like 30 songs on it," Manning reveals. "It had a cover that was soon [complained] about. We released ten or twenty like that, then twenty with a different cover. It had songs "Like Baby I Love You," "I Hate Cops," "EPA," "Wall of Doom," "Monologue Song," and "Trigger Happy." We only did songs a couple times since we were always writing new stuff [about] something I wanted said or was pissed about. I could write what I wanted, and they could put music to it ... When we went to Studio B in 1987 to record, the engineer was very religious but recorded us anyway. He changed our name on the bill and said he tried slowing the tracks down after we left to see if he could figure out what I was singing about. That, my friend, is priceless."

Bludgeoned Nun was featured in the second issue of my zine *No Deposit No Return* when local authorities began threatening to close down clubs where the band played. The piece read: "This ban on Bludgeoned Nun is the second to happen in this town but the first to come from the mayor and his harem of neo-fascist aldermen and be enforced by the local goon squad." Due to some members' shaved heads and scuffed, laced-up boots, they were stigmatized locally as unwanted cretins and teenage menaces. Yet, they were not anything like the skinheads that appeared in the late 1980s and early 1990s on a tide of misplaced Aryan pride.

The early skinheads, like bass player Jeff Gresenz, soon grew out their hair within a few years, dropped the suspenders, and listened to the Replacements and Steve Earle. Meanwhile, Bludgeoned Nun took a staunch anti-Nazi stance. As they stated in their interview with me, their potent sarcasm, social critiques, speed-infused thrash, and anti-religious fervor was fueled by a fight against "an army of uniformed neo-Nazi mindless zombies chanting Bible verses." To illustrate their sound, they described, "Jerry Falwell singing the 'Old Rugged Cross' while Tammy Baker pulls out his pubic hairs one by one." In songs and—interviews, they attacked church, media, and conformity, both in the mainstream and underground community.

Manning continued to ply his trade locally in Rockford as national, melodic, and commercially viable "hardcore" punk like the Offspring and Pennywise became the norm. "My second band was eventually called Maggot Plate. We did it for the fun of it ... The third band was The Apostles of Gein. After going to shows for a while with Rick and seeing what was being classed as punk or hardcore, we decided we had to start a band and kick the scene in the ass. We had a couple lineup changes until we got what we wanted to make our sound heard." With surefire agility, the band melded paired-down metallic riffage, tempo-changing chops, adrenalin-spiked speed, crust-punk looks, and dark subject matter to make any Accused or Doom fan shudder with adoration.

The band gigged in nearby towns and landed two songs on the Black and Blue Records compilation *Music to Make Your Ears Hurt Too*. They signed to Beer City Records after a show at the PIT in Rockford, releasing a 7" record and receiving offers to tour with shock punkers the Murder Junkies. "I loved doing this band—great chemistry—and our sound was evolving ... Though we had plans to release another 7", due to personal reasons we just broke up and went our ways. In Apostles, we hit on a lot of stuff that we did not in Nun.

Black Sunday Black Sunday Black Sunday Black Sunday
IT'S TIME FOR PEACE NOT WAR

Maggot Plate had some songs that still make me glad ... The way I always looked at it: say what's on your mind, make people think and question things, and anything said about you in a band is [illuminating], no matter if it's good or bad. I just found it funny to see people get worked up over a band name or a song title. Hell, half the time you could not understand the lyrics anyway." As so many bands—especially of the d-beat and crust genres—know well, their band names and song titles alone were enough to earn them condemnation. Meanwhile, most outsiders could barely make out their gruff vocals, which often acted as a code that only insiders—those with their ears attentively pasted to the aural grime—could unlock and translate. To casual listeners, it usually amounted to vociferous noise pollution.

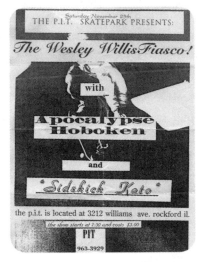

Other local underground music veterans of the time included We Hate Cake, who played the same circuit of rented halls and Rotation Station. "There is a mythology in Rockford that we were the original hardcore punk band in town, but we were just sloppy rock'n'roll," admits drummer Stu Patterson, who played on the demo tape *No One Takes Care of Me* featuring tunes like "Ginger Lynn," "Kill F.M." and "No More Parties." "Bill Dolan was thirteen, I think, when we started, so there was a heavy learning curve for all of us. I had played in a few bar bands, so I was probably more experienced than the other guys, but my playing level had reached a plateau of 'slightly above average mediocrity,' and they soon surpassed my abilities. I think I only played four or five shows with them. We opened for Die Kreuzen and the Descendents at 229 Club and some other touring bands before I quit."

Under-aged guitarist Bill Dolan was a seminal figure in the nascent all-ages punk scene of the 1980s. Early on, he joined peer Chris Nilsson in the creation of the fanzine *Protest and Survive*, which later attracted friend Kurt Niesman as well. As Dolan recalls, "Chris's dad had a Xerox machine in their basement ... a super early model copy machine that could only print on one side of paper, and the print was not super good." The trio printed "four pages of adolescent banter ... surely not worth any higher minded person's reading time." Like hundreds, perhaps thousands, of other youth producing similar spontaneous, off-the-cuff, low-tech, self-made publications across the rapidly booming fanzine nation, they mixed light-hearted zeal with genre obsessions. "We had an article about Black Flag growing their hair out. We were saying that it was not punk rock to have long hairdos. We were being silly, of course, and being obnoxious about it too."

"The joyful act of making a fanzine could create conversations, prove the authenticity of a local punk, or even garner respect from jaded locals. This is how I met Chris 'Buzzsaw' Gaffney and Scott Thompson, and how we started We Hate Cake. Through this fanzine, I became acquainted with 'Norway Rat' (Dwight Gail) and 'Unisex' Nicole Diventi too. Buzzsaw and Scott were a bit older and more well-versed in English punk but also American acts that Chris, Kurt, and I were not yet listening to. Scott Thompson was frequently talking about [British punk icons] UK Subs, Stiff Little Fingers, and Peter and The Test Tube Babies. Meanwhile, Buzzsaw was often promoting [American punk and raucous rock'n'roll via] the Plasmatics, the Stooges, Alice Cooper, and the Ramones, of course. I was into the Ramones, Sex Pistols, and Dead Kennedys, but I had not heard much of these previously mentioned Punk Rock acts."

Hence, one issue of a fanzine could act like a gateway. In this case, the three "editors" would quickly become an ingrained part of the musical landscape of the city both via the fanzine and the demo tape by their band Aerosol Vomit in Rockford, which amounted to an excursion by Dolan (alias Pop Guru), Nilsson (alias X Lax), and Niesman (alias

Norman Lyric) into filth and fury. Like their punk forbearers (Cheetah Chrome, Johnny Rotten, John Doe, etc.), the kids used smart-ass aliases to cloak their identities. "The lyrics were graphic and vile because that's what punk was when you're fourteen," admits Niesman. "We knowingly ripped off Dead Kennedys, Bowie, and the Cramps, basically copying whatever we knew at the time, which in my case was very little. Bill was making tape edits from a children's

record and using haunted house sounds too." The band managed to cut a demo, "Spontaneous Garbage," in 1984, but then stalled out. Dolan began slinging his guitar in We Hate Cake and War on the Saints, but those bang-em-out cursory songs were ready for a second life.

"In 1988, I purchased a cassette four track, which opened *everything* up," says Niesman. Aerosol Vomit cut a new demo, "Swingers Lingo," using a drum machine and lassoing Dolan back in after his hiatus (who is dressed as a Gene Simmons from KISS caricature on the demo cover art), then hooked up with drummer Ted Cahill. They lost none of their tongue-in-cheek methods, which made them closer to Ween than the Exploited. "Somehow we opened for [earnest melodic hardcore band] Dag Nasty as Aerosol Vomit. It was the height of non-seriousness," Niesman notes. "I dressed like Axl Rose by wearing a sleeveless E'I'E'I'O' shirt, and we had back-up lady dancers. Dag Nasty's guitarist Brian Baker asked me afterwards if we had written those songs in second grade. I told him it was seventh."

That rampant mockery and fun was worn like a second skin, even as they morphed into the new unit Becky's Birthday and gigged with national acts. "We thought pissing off punkers was punker than dogmatic leather jackets and tempo breakdowns," insists Niesman. "And it made us laugh. For the Fugazi gig, we embraced more of a classic rock bent. I think we opened with a Bad Company song and took the inserts of a live Journey record and taped pictures of the members on the amps, drums, and mic stands. Bill even burned incense during the set." In this way, they created a punk situation rather than mirror punk's somewhat narrow musicality, then began to shift to more serious ground as sincere Soul Asylum worshippers.

Their approach was quite similar to the DIY punk formula replicated throughout the world: grab an instrument, experiment with your early teen notions of piled-up angst, then grow into something more mature—a band with more fluid and focused sets, but not overly serious or planned. Back then, genre conventions seemed unbound, porous, and gray. Bands like Aerosol Vomit and Becky's Birthday figured out their musical trademarks on the fly, and kept the fun intact.

Plus, they honed skill sets for the future, attests Niesman. "I'm floored by the amount of time and skills we put into this ... learning typesetting, Xerox manipulation, crafting artwork mock-ups, and more ... We literally made a can of Aerosol Vomit, complete with pea soup puke and American cheese, just so we could take a picture and then go get it developed then paste it onto paper in order to be Xeroxed." In this sense, the band's hands-on aesthetics likely made them closer to Andy Warhol's The Factory than to bands lining the shelves of Hot Topic years later.

Dolan and Gaffney would reappear and unite briefly in a band called Speck with Jeff Gresenz and Stu Patterson. "I remember a particularly gruesome gig at Rotation Station. Kids were literally running/skating away from the band as a rumor spread through the crowd that Chris was tripping on acid and was going to kill himself or someone in the audience! Of course, he was just drunk as usual," says Patterson. "We recorded a demo. It was pretty awful, but I heard a rumor that someone put out a single from those recordings. Like I said, I'm doubtful that is real, but weirder things have happened." That unit soon imploded.

Like much of the U.S., skateboarding was the backbone of the 1980s Rockford underground music scene, Vince Jumapao, singer of War on the Saints, avows. The skate scene attracted people far and wide across the disparate city, plus it spurred music, artwork, and camaraderie among the "degenerates," who congregated at various social hubs, including Toad Hall, a two-story dilapidated storefront-cum-home filled to the brim with dust-mottled poetry, cheap western paperbacks, Hollywood movie posters, and racks of LPs—mostly a dime-a-dozen pop detritus. Yet, a rare Ramones, Decry, or Social Distortion LP gave punks hope, plus the low-lit cellar teemed with scratched 45s, including an occasional cut by 1960s neanderthal garage rockers the Troggs or even 1970s art-rockers Magazine.

Businesses that combined jaw-dropping skate ramps and raucous live music, like Rotation Station and the PIT, would not have existed without hundreds of edgy kids flocking to them. Some of the early scenesters first tested their audacious skills at the Barn, owned by Erik Evanson, whose family had lived on the property since the 1800s. Secretly hidden away, it featured a full pipe ramp, which empowered and catalyzed the kids, who learned quickly to skate at advanced levels and become full-on pros or at least audacious, adept skater punks who could shred endlessly. Even Warren "Torch" DeMartini, from the metal band Ratt, was at the Barn one night because he was high school friends with one of the regulars.

In 1984, Chris Furney zoomed to California for Christmas vacation and brought back a copy of skate magazine *Thrasher*, brimming with adverts for Kyptonics, Dogtown, Santa Cruz, and the *Skate Rock* compilation series, to his cohort of pals, including Jumapao. From the newsprint, they gleaned information about bands like Metallica, still a garage metal band at the time, and Dead Kennedys, while also reading descriptive, salivating reviews by Pushead. Soon, the scene began to gestate a more skatecore side due to the enthusiasm and commitment of locals like Jumapao.

During one fiery We Hate Cake performance at Rotation Station, singer Chris "Buzzsaw"

Insight, Madison, 1988

Gaffney stomped off the stage, snapped his mic stand in two, told everyone "fuck you, fuck off" while cupping his hand around his mouth, and stormed outside to swallow gulps of Bacardi rum. Gaffney hated the band's new musical formula and they had apparently broken up onstage. Chris seemed to stir an air of violence. "There was a group of kids that listened to Depeche Mode and lifted weights. They just didn't like Chris as he was quick to make fun of them and others of their ilk," attests drummer Stu Patterson. "They cornered him in the parking lot after we played 229 Club one time and beat him pretty severely. The cops showed up right away, but Chris was hurt pretty bad. He and I spent the rest of the night at the ER."

In the mid-1980s, Kevin Hutchins was a metalhead dreaming of wild-eyed success behind his kit, but an accident altered his course. While showering in his parents' basement shower, the plate glass at the bottom shattered, so "the top plate slid down and guillotined my right foot. It severed all tendons, nerves, and two arteries. I nearly bled to death as I was rushed to the emergency room," tells Hutchins. Even after a two-hour surgery and two months in a cast, the doctor doubted his ability to walk again.

During that time, his drum skills altered. "I used my left foot instead of my right. When I fully recovered with my right foot, I had developed a unique strength and style using my double bass pedal." Hutchins was also dating a girl whose sister scoured the 229 Club/Channels scene and dated Gary from Bludgeoned Nun. "They had no place to practice, so her parents let them use their basement. I heard all of their practices, dug it, and found out they needed a drummer, and was actually thinking about joining..."

Yet, a knock on the Hutchins' door changed everything. "There was a guy there with a leather coat with chains all over it wearing red plaid pants and short, spiked hair, a kind of punk look handed down from 1977. "Are you Kevin?" I replied, "Yeah." The guy said, "You play drums, right?" I said, "Yeah." "You want to join a band?" I said "Sure." He handed me a tape and told me to learn the songs and give him a call back, if interested. I looked at the tape, 'WE HATE CAKE!' Fuck! It was the rival band of Bludgeoned Nun that was practicing in my fucking girlfriend's basement!" Rockford was a small turf, so looking back in hindsight such agitation and animosity likely represented a day-by-day, gig-by-gig struggle for the hearts and minds of a small hive of punk followers. "I remember hearing her say, 'That's going to go over

well,'" says Hutchins. "I still to this day don't know how Scott knew I was even a drummer, let alone was interested in joining a band ... or where I lived." In the end, Hutchins did not receive flak for being in We Hate Cake either.

Hutchins loved the We Hate Cake tape, especially the speed, to which he could apply fast double bass patterns. Members Scott Thompson, Chris "Buzzsaw" Gaffney, and Bill Dolan were high school rebels. Guitarist Bill Dolan offered agility, bassist Scott Thompson used melodic hooks that danced around Bill's unique guitar style, and Buzzsaw, a poet and artist, occupied a different planet.

A couple of gigs after Hutchins joined, Buzzsaw flopped on the ground in the middle of a set, failed to get up during a song, and missed his vocal cue. A heated argument erupted between Buzzsaw and bass player Thompson.

Afterwards, guitarist Bill Dolan talked to skater Vince Jumapao (who never sang before) into fronting War on the Saints, according to Hutchins.

Buzzsaw tended to burn his bridges; he was a tempestuous character. *Maximum Rock'n'roll* "depressed" him, and he had little regard for bands like Dead Kennedys, Dolan remembers. With his MC5 shirt hung loose and a bottle of cheap beer in his hand, he could be a walking maelstrom, but people loved his dark humor, his confrontational honesty, and his Charles Bukowski-inspired street verse. But the band thrived without him.

"Vince Jumapao packed an amazing voice and became a very talented writer. Soon, the direction of the music was more of a 'thinking man's, progressive, alternative style' instead of just 'punk,'" says Hutchins. "The bonus? Vince also brought 350 of his best skate punk friends to pack the fucking house every time we played."

Guitarist Bill Dolan had other plans too: he had been sending demos to labels. "He came to us with a publishing deal/recording contract with Kevin Second's label Positive Force Records," Hutchins reveals, so we recorded our six-song self-titled EP with Dan Kubinski from Die Kreuzen on backup vocals. During the recording, "Bill was discouraged with Vince and wanted to replace him with Dan from Die Kreuzen," and after the tracks were completed, Dolan left to rejoin Aerosol Vomit/ Becky's Birthday.

During this period, Phil Drucker formed the new record label White Hat Records/Good Guise/Road Kill Records with Garrison White, who took notice of War on the Saints's tours of the Midwest and their follow-up to the EP, a full-length CD called *Whoyamakinhappy?* recorded at

IDFUL Studios in Chicago. Drucker sent the session master tapes to Germany to release as an import and promised a U.S.A. release too, which fizzled. "Now and then we see that ... it hit radio charts too, but we took a break from it all, though still remain friends and dabble with an occasional reunion," says Hutchins. Their lasting legacy is more nuanced, though. "We really were the only Alternative, Post-Punk, Pre-Grunge, Progressive Rock band..." he notes, meaning the band rose above punk platitudes and three chord clichés. This might not have appealed to the rank and file underground, but it signaled their willingness to adapt, grow, and morph with the times.

During this era, Chris Furney, whose *Thrasher* fanzines had inspired Vince Jumapao, began to attend the small, Lutheran-affiliated Augustana College along the Illinois/Iowa borderland, but soon moved home and became a show promoter, photographer, and poetic singer of Insight. "I started in the band hoping that if we were to get out in the public arena we could get an intelligent message out, make a difference, so we try to do just that," Furney wrote in *Word* fanzine in a profile about Insight. "I'd like to think music is like books and pamphlets are to a revolution; if more bands were to try and say something, maybe eventually some sort of act will be made on the issues we sing about." On the Insight tune "What I Have," he explored scripture and war: "Where is the glory / in gunning down a man / for the sake of religions / or 'cause he takes a different stand." In the aforementioned fanzine piece, he also admits the band tended to be influenced by post-hardcore Washington D.C. bands and second wave New York hardcore bands like Gorilla Biscuits and Underdog. To pay honor to those roots, Insight covered "Never Go Back" by Dag Nasty, whose propulsive rhythms, melodic but jet-fueled strenuous hardcore, and dripping-with-nostalgia vocals made sense to us as we began to grow, mature, and explore different musical possibilities.

"That was an amazing time in my life," admits Jeremy Kunz. "We used to go out all night and plaster posters for upcoming punk rock shows all over Rockford, as if anyone driving down Main Street by the downtown bridges was actually going to be able to read those fliers as they drove by at 45 miles an hour! But we had fun doing it. Also, Operation Ivy playing in my basement while my dad was away on business was great. My mom and sister were handing out snacks to kids between songs, who were slam dancing in my childhood home. I was sixteen years old!"

After other shows, NOFX mocked the veggie frozen pizza and SNFU hammered around on the exercise equipment in front of my camera lens. "It was a blast!" Kunz enthuses. "So young and free and ambitious for punk rock." His mother was patient, selfless, and supportive. Punk tours happened not because of just scribbled phone numbers, gas guzzling cars, and dingy clubs, but because punks could literally crash on dog hair smattered couches and pick through refrigerators; punk was often a family affair, if your parents didn't kick you out to the curb.

Another key figure was Weasel Walters, whose love of confrontation and a mix of heady art rock like PiL (the post-Sex Pistols band of Johnny Rotten/Lydon) and free jazz pioneer Albert Ayler led him to form Chernobyl Chyldren with Erik Byrne, whose sister Amy recalls, "I thought he and his friends were the biggest bunch of weirdoes around! I thought they looked like freaks with the hair and clothes. But then I listened to the music, and it touched a part of me I didn't even know I had. Bands like The Clash—still my favorite to this day, Sex Pistols, Bad Brains, The Damned, and more spoke to me from the inside out. Before I knew it, I was one of those weirdoes with strange hair, clothes, makeup, and jewelry!"

At thirteen years old, Erik gelled with Walters, a few years younger, and Cip Jumapao (brother of Vince), so they tried igniting a band. At the time, a version of Bludgeoned Nun with Gary Manning (who married Amy Byrne for a time) missing in action was looking for a drummer during the summer of 1985. "Glen, the guitarist, tried to show me how to play 'hardcore drums', but I didn't get it," Erik recalls. "The next year Weasel and I kept in touch and started Chernobyl Chyldren." Weasel took on the bass duties, Erik hammered out his own style on drums, and they found some willing partners in their creative crimes. "We practiced anywhere we could and played a few basement shows and one at Rotation Station." Like many other young bands, especially in Rockford, the lineup switched, the band eked out a demo, and then the unit imploded. "Jeremy Kunts, Weasel, and I stayed together and started the Javelin Bats. This must have been '86 or '87: we did New York style no-wave stuff and recorded endlessly with stolen gear we took from our high school's 'radio club.' I still have a bunch of the demos we made, and it captures the three of us learning different instruments as we'd switch off instruments out of either boredom or just being able to play better on different songs."

Just as the first wave of Rockford punks utilized their high school friends, talent contests, and radio stations as a means to foster their own laboratory of learning, so did the hardcore kids, even if by means of furtive theft. The hardcore generation was not simple cut-n-paste formula followers of the music from every major metropolis. They were restless, inventive, sometimes even hostile to trends, and sought new forms to express themselves. Though Weasel was the son of a firefighter, and Erik drove around in a compact truck like any welder in town, they merged the spirit of 1976-1980 in New York City, when no-waver Lydia Lunch brutally caterwauled and James Chance deconstructed funk and white angst. Rockford's scene was somehow diverse, antsy, and by no means homogenized.

After graduation, Walters immigrated to Chicago and formed the much-lauded noise-jazz-punk outfit the Flying Luttenbachers. Meanwhile, Erik formed the Reacharounds. One gig featured the band taking center stage at a downtown rollerskating rink. "For my 25th birthday we rented out the entire place including all skate rentals," tells Erik. "They still had a functioning *Saturday Night Fever* light up disco dance floor, so that's where the band set up. They let us bring in a keg of beer, but we couldn't tap it until all the skates were turned back in. It was a hilariously fun time watching all the punks roller skating with Mohawks and leather jackets on!"

In terms of heavy, instrumental riffage, the obscure but powerful Here gigged intermittently, including noted Rockford skateboarder Brad Burnell, drummer Stu Patterson, and sound engineer Scott Colborn. Burnell also played on the local 7" single by Rod Myers & The Ramps, dubbed "dis-abilly" because Rod was a disabled rocker. "He would come over to Brad Burnell's occasionally when I lived over there," Patterson remembers. "The song 'Wheelchair' was done to the tune of 'Wild Thing', the video of which was featured on *Real People*, a primetime TV show."

One of Burnell's cohorts was the ever-shifting Adam Becvare, whose career has been a dizzying route through underground music, including a friendship with Brian James of the Damned and Lords of the New Church. "The Lords had me fill in for Stiv since '03 until now, including an album and touring." Meanwhile, Becvare also appeared on the latest Brian James Gang release with punk veteran Cheetah Chrome of Dead Boys.

Yet, his path to working with such legends almost seems pre-destined, for he learned much of their scorching songs as a skinny teen coping with life at suburban Guilford High School, whose hallways also hosted the aforementioned Louie Name, and the high-wired, brazen likes of Don Bush and Ronnie Falls: "They were good-looking guys and had bands and parties on Sunnyside Dr ... Their bands started luring all the girls the jocks tried to follow, which made for bad brawls. I moved in with them at sixteen. These were the guys that taught me Vibrators, Dolls, Clash, Dead Boys, and Gen X. Their bands were Deadline, Hep Boy, etc. which often played covers ranging from the Ramones and New York Dolls to UFO and Aerosmith." In the 1980s, such bleed over between metal and punk was not uncommon, especially in smaller towns.

"I had always grown up with the raw sound of the punk music," says Falls, bass player for the Unspeakables and 3 Songs Too Many, "but it all really started to be real at Sunnyside Dr. This opened up a whole new world. All of sudden I was living the punk scene: four guys lived in a house, which soon fell into pure destruction. The house may have taken the best of all of us." Like so many other punks, Falls' crew took a communal approach, which began as a means to save and split rent money, practice their rock'n'roll licks with abandon, but it also become a black hole of sorts, a Dionysian den. From the loft parties of Manhattan in the 1970s to the house party DIY spirit of this millennium, such places have always been part of punk lore.

And like so many others, first these roommates sharpened their skills on the canon: "It wasn't long before we started putting songs together, a set list composed of the likes of Dead Boys, Circle Jerks, Dead Kennedys, Clash, Ramones, Wire, Sex Pistols, Plasmatics, Lords of the New Church, Gen X, Black Flag, Agent Orange. The list went on—most with three chord power chords, nasty, raw vocals, buzzing guitar, and a drummer that couldn't be stopped." The band regularly gigged at the Deli, as well as parties. When they ventured to Beloit, WI, fisticuffs ensued. "We got banned from bars because we were too loud and obnoxious. One in particular was Le Club. We ended up writing a song called "Banned From Le Club": "Ban ban ban ban, you punks, are drunks, you're banned from Le Club." Just like the Bad Brains were banned from Washington D.C., The Germs and Black Flag were banned from clubs in L.A., they were banned too. In a way, such treatment became a punk badge of honor. A band branded as too intense, too renegade, too unmanageable, too outlaw, was indeed a truly hardcore band.

Falls' inebriated revelry kicked into high gear. "Sunnyside Dr., which should have been labeled Suicide Dr., was soon the place to be on the weekends. It started with fellow punkers, both male and female, but soon spread to the popular girls, which soon brought the jocks in: it was off the charts, wall-to-wall. People usually would end up with squad cars and kids scrambling not to get busted for underage drinking." In the 1970s and 80s, that was typical fare for rock'n'roll youth of all stripes, but this scene became more mired in punk degeneracy than *16 Candles* or *The Breakfast Club*.

The dust would settle momentarily, but soon parties would erupt, again awash in drugs and alcohol. The environment became overtly destructive; the house started showing real signs of an unstoppable force, and not just from punk rock, but petty criminality as well, Falls recalls. "Holes were in the drywalls not only from combat boots and fists but gunshots and homemade nunchucks too, doors were ripped off all the bedrooms and sheets hung up in their place, carpets were filled with puke, urine, and blood stains, and who knows what else. Dirty dishes piled up in the sink for weeks. Most of the time we would toss them out in a big garbage can. One afternoon, I awoke to a house of massive amounts of food, hairspray, toothpaste, and cigarettes. Another band member raided a local grocery store and hooked our starving asses up. Stuff was everywhere. I have no idea how he did all that by himself. He ended up in jail for a few weeks, only to return to see that we had consumed it all."

The strangest part, though, might have been their cleaning lady. "A four foot Italian grandma would come over, and all you hear is a broom sweeping beer cans and bottles and her mumbling nasty words about us. She used a broom to clean the carpet because the vacuum would not cut through dampness." But even she could not sterilize the place. "It all came to an end when one of the band members decided to play with a razor blade, came out of the bathroom bleeding, had another band member grab an old dirty sock from the rank carpet, wrap it around him, and sent him to the ambulance. All I could think was 'infection for sure,' for that sock had been there a week or so."

These were the last gasps of the Sunnyside era, which seemed like a punk version of the seediness one expected from portions of the derelict downtown, with its filigree of flea bag resident hotels and dank porno stall gloryholes.

"In a way, people like Falls taught me everything I shouldn't do in life," Becvare avows. "They were always 86'd from parties and bars because their ideas of a good time mostly meant being jackasses. Drinking'n'fights galore ... outrageous times," Becvare recalls. "When I was thirteen, Doug was my guitar teacher." In the days when rock'n'roll genres were more fluid and gray, "he would play Randy Rhoads (Ozzy Osbourne) and Judas Priest licks, then send me home with the Dead

Boys and Clash. Craig Emerson, quite the brawler, was a great drummer then." All that rambunctious irreverence and steady diet of song fueled Becvare's own ambitions.

"At sixteen, I played for RIPT at the Sinnissippi Park bandshell. But I left metal for a new wave project—In the Pink—with Gordy Cushman and Matt Lentz (known in the media as Matthew Roberts, son of Charles Manson) as well as Hep Boy. They were the older punks. I was an understudy. Their guitarist had slashed his wrist." As Becvare tells, "Out of Order ... were a high school cover band that played lots of house parties and jammed the Romantics, Cheap Trick, the Cult, Billy Idol, and the Ramones—the cool, radio friendlies. I refused photos for my 1986 Guilford senior yearbook. But I'm told they sent someone to a show and used those. I've never seen it, though. Should be priceless!"

Adam sought to push beyond the borders of Rockford. "I moved to Los Angeles to play with post-Ted Nugent Damn Yankees that became rockers Kills for Thrills, but I left rock for goth and returned to Rockford for the Wake, then industrial with Sex Trip Netwerk with John Soroka [who played with Ministry]" who also migrated to Chicago. "Then I relearned guitar, went back to punk, while grunge had the world by the throat, in Buick MacKane and The Drill, which lasted locally until 1994, then moved to New York City to join Control, which featured Anthony Esposito of Lynch Mob and Ace Frehley of KISS. I toured greaser punk networks with The Heartdrops from New York City, but left them to tour with Marky Ramone, but couldn't get a visa."

I stumbled upon Becvare while exiting a restaurant in the night-swollen city of Manhattan in 1996. Both of us had left Rockford, attempted to find our place in rock'n'roll's juggernaut cultural landscape, and had succeeded, though in small steps.

Trenchmouth, Alumni House

FLAC, CBGB, NYC

Four
DECONSTRUCTING THE
DECADENT 1990S

Many scenesters jettisoned Rockford in the early 1990s and zoomed west. After dropping out of a college and university, I finished community college and headed to Santa Fe; longtime show promoter and singer Tad Keyes and bass player Erik Byrne drifted to Minneapolis, and others landed in Los Angeles. Punk music, like the scene, was in transition. The Epitaph/Fat Wreck Chords/Lookout generation began to ascend swiftly. Bands like Bad Religion and NOFX had labored for years on the road, paying dues, then created impressive, dynamic studio albums that fused insistent melody and zealous speed. Meanwhile, punk seemed to become mainstream overnight as audiences eagerly latched onto a more produced version of the bands and scene that had nurtured us. Simultaneously going deeper underground, the noise, powerviolence, screamo, gunk and garage rock, and Riot Grrrl scenes thrived too.

To critics, like a college friend of mine who witnessed the last show of Boston art-punk missionaries Mission of Burma in the 1980s, much of the radio-friendly punk, such as Green Day and Blink-182, came across as hollow and safe pop music. Plus, the niche markets of the underground DIY scene seemed equally problematic, as if all tiers of punk had become overrun by the free-market enterprise. Punk consumers took on the collecting nature of comic book nerds, memorizing how many copies of each record were made of each edition in each color. Was the sleeve hand-printed by stencil and spraypaint? Was the vinyl a dense palette of non-black colors? Did it come with inserts, stickers and a catalog? Was it numbered by hand? Knowing and evaluating such painstaking minutiae placed buyers—and hoarders—within a social stratum of collectors, even as heavyweight punk rockers Poison Idea mocked them a decade earlier in their EP titled *Record Collectors Are Prententious Assholes.*

One aspect no one could doubt: punk was burgeoning, exploding, and once again taking the land by storm.

Locally, just like my old cohorts, a handful of people became the newest Do-It-Yourself crew in town by maintaining a new circuit of spaces and indoor skate parks, creating record labels, and forging music that matched the times. By the early 1990s, the band **FLAC** mobilized a new generation of youth living along the Wisconsin and Illinois borderline. Musician Brad Towell, only fourteen years old when he frenetically plucked bass in Insight, led the way, and Paul Deuth eventually joined on guitar. **FLAC** was a tight, genre-bending, self-reliant unit that organized shows under the moniker Tinnitus. "Jeff Weeter did most of the booking and logistics," tells Towell. "I did most of the design and promotions. Playing with Alice Donut, Victims Family, and Giant Metal Insects was a huge moment for us. Jeff and Jenn Weeter's Mom, Pat, made dinner for everyone before the show. We all ate chili at the Alumni house. It was an amazing time in our lives."

Due to sheer talent, pragmatic sensibilities, supportive families, and burning desire, bands like **FLAC** were able to help incubate a whole era that was not dependent upon bars and clubs. "It was the DIY spirit that really drove us," drummer Weeter avows. "Speaking for myself, I wanted to put on shows with bands I wanted to see and perform with. We had to make our own scene complete with strange production companies and record labels. I wrote to Dischord and Alternative Tentacles back then and received loads of great info on how to make records and other tips. It was really inspiring stuff. FLAC's 7" was produced using Dischord's suggested pressing plant and Brad's amazing graphics. There was even a promotional version made with a silk-screened box. The band and the scene around it was a really great way to push one's ideas and make them materialize. Hugely influential for me as a teen."

The PIT, another nexus of skateboarding and edge sports culture, became an epicenter of the 1990s scene in Rockford, fueled by SN Productions, the efforts of Tom Williams and Dan Garrison.

Occasional headaches and tumult got stirred up at the PIT. Jack Grisham, legendary punk singer of TSOL, was performing with his new band the Joykiller. Grisham seemed to scuffle with a teenager due to the kid's fanzine diatribe against major labels, which irked the veteran punk. "After major apologies from the booking agent, but not Jack, I agreed to have Joykiller play again. Not a lot of people attended," Williams recalls, "but those that did appeared bent on revenge. Fireworks were lit at them while on stage." Kids threw things at Grisham, and, "He was called a bully and a piece of shit by the kids ... but Jack brought it on himself. This was the point where I started to think about quitting." Such occurrences certainly fray one's nerves and make one question the whole point of maintaining shows, but Williams was able to see the misadventure from several angles.

"I look at it like this. I know the road life is a struggle," Williams admits. "You've given up your life to play. You show up and there's a kid putting your band down for the label you are on. Aggression from struggling and being belittled took over. Not a good excuse, but I can understand. When Down by Law played, they were a wreck. Money and van problems had them stressed. Still, Dave and the guys still had high spirits. I paid for a new alternator and installed it in their van in the parking lot. I missed most of the show and was done about ten minutes before they went on. The gratitude and their generosity showed me there are good people in bands. Some days I do miss it all. If I had the time I'd do it all again. The good and the bad." Just like members of Youth of Today stopped by to play basketball in the front of my house, or bands lounged exhausted in the basement of Kunz's, Williams's diligence and help was actively creating a sense of community that made punk *not* business as usual.

Another notorious night, according to PIT regulars, included an ill-attended gig by punk legacy act Fear (whose contract insisted on St. Pauli Girl Beer), which included singer Lee Ving taking off his belt and threatening to pummel the promoter, shoving a back stage fan, punching a young man to the floor, being spat on by locals while on stage, and jumping in the van after only a few songs.

In a more playful, separate manner, Wesley Willis—outsider musician, prolific artist, and diagnosed schizophrenic—rabidly head-butted his fans at his gig. "I am one of the few people who never got head-butted by Wesley," remembers Amy Byrne. "He was head-butting everyone and came near to me. I gave him the 'Mom Look' and told him he had better not even try. He looked into my eyes, nodded his head, and steered clear of me forever after!" That's what made the era so unpredictable. One night a ska band would make the kids skank, and on another they might shrink away from the likes of Willis, whose physicality was even more intense and unpredictable than a stopover gig by a third generation spiky haired punk squad.

In 1991, Green Day was supposed to appear at Denzil's Music Emporium, just minutes away from their gig venue in Beloit, for an afternoon meet and greet with fans. But as Barb Orr recalls, a mini-disaster ensued. "They never showed. They were always on board with the idea ... until that particular day. This was *way* before they were featured on MTV, and the only fan base they had was built on their live shows and their reviews in zines like *MRR*. It was built due to college radio play and indie record stores like Denzil's." Despite depending on such a backbone of support, the band blew off the 50 fans that flocked to the tiny store on the main drag and sat around, chewing pizza and taking turns on the free arcade game.

"I was thinking that they had gotten a late start," Orr admits, "that they got hung up in traffic, that they were hung over. Although any of those three possibilities are still plausible, it turned out to be much worse. When Billie Joe [Armstrong] took the stage at The Hangout, he started with a spoken word. Unequivocally, he informed everyone in the crowd that 'autograph signing is sell-out bullshit!!!' He then ranted, 'FUCK Denzil's! It's just corporate BULLSHIT! Don't ever buy one of our records there!'"

Little did the loudmouth singer know that Denzil, the owner of the store, was recording the show off the soundboard. "He was shocked and hurt and angry," says Orr. "I'm pretty sure he threw that recording away."

The band's set did shred in the sweat-caked venue and Orr decided to seize the moment after the last distorted chord dissipated. "I approached Mister Bille Joe and politely requested to speak with him outside. All hell broke loose, and he deserved it." As Orr turned up the heat on him, she explained one simple fact. "Denzil's was the *only* independent record store in Beloit, and I ordered most of the punk inventory." Up on the stage, fully ranting in an ignorant monologue, he had "basically just told everyone to go shop at Musicland," insists Orr.

She lost her cool, admonishing him: "Is *that* what you fucking want?!!"

Billie Joe apologized for the snafu in the parking lot. "We came to terms that pretty much everyone on earth has the potential to be a dick, so who can you really trust?" Orr says. After the tense stand-off, Armstrong eventually "played 'Blue Moon' on acoustic and sang it, while James 'Brainstew' Washburn thumped out a rhythm on the hood of the van in the parking lot," she recalls, which became a public service announcement for WBCR: "Hello, I'm Billie Joe from Green Day, and you're listening to WBCR."

Still, despite the peace gesture, the damage was done. Some heroes deflate within seconds.

Orr decided to give the band the benefit of the doubt and booked them on her own in the summer of 1992. "We had agreed, months in advance, to a guaranteed amount of $400 for this show. At that time, it was a generous amount for a three-piece touring band. I had always prided myself on paying the two opening acts $200 each, while biting my nails and being hopeful that my promotion would turn heads and make people leave their houses to attend a small all-ages venue." Like many women of her generation, Orr was not content to sit in the shadows. She took DIY to heart.

She rented the venue, the stage, the lights, and promised to pay the sound man; no small feat for any young person. "It was always a bit terrifying, knowing that I was on the line to be sure that everyone was paid what they were promised. During the show, I had to leave the door (and more importantly the till) to tend to an issue. When I returned, the door was unmanned, and the till was, unsurprisingly, empty."

Undeterred, she did not cave in, she problem-solved. Luckily, she had kept track of the cash amount formerly on-hand and knew how to act quickly. "I enlisted a more trustworthy friend to watch the door and sped off to Denzil's, taking out a loan from the cash register in the amount that had gone missing. SHIT SHIT! It took me all summer to pay that off."

But that loss was nothing compared to her newest Armstrong melee about to occur.

"Billie Joe and I exchanged the agreed $400 in the parking lot. At this point, he lost *his* cool! He thought that I had hidden money from them," she recalls, "and they deserved to be paid more than previously agreed."

"Everyone has the potential to be a dick" rang in her thoughts. That dose of reality quickly rose to the surface, again.

"I lost my cool, marched inside, returned with a $20 bill, and handed it to him. He proceeded to crumple it up and throw it in my face! What ensued makes me chuckle to this day: Two people (one of whom is now substantially wealthier than the other) screaming at one another and throwing a wadded $20 bill back and forth, back and forth. He called me a bitch, and I called him an asshole."

Years later, she rescinds none of the story but also embraces the experiences: "They formed my view of the underground punk scene, the corporate music industry and (most importantly) a person's potential ... Just depends upon what kind of person you are potentially trying to be at that given moment in time. Sure, people grow, mature, have children, and carve careers on the back of the punk underground, but some scars don't disappear. Those moments can't be erased. Like many of us who worked with punk icons, our feelings were often shattered by some of the experiences. The faults of well-known punks often ran just as deep as other petulant 'stars.'"

One of the ground-level local leaders in the era was tough-skinned pop punk Mulligan Stu, led by singer/guitarist Kevin Kalen. The band was prodigious and appeared on a flexi 7" with Less than Jake and Boris the Sprinkler titled *Defender of the Rock'n'Roll Universe,* a split 7" with Teen Idols, and made the album *Do The Kids Wanna Rock?* The band embodied the work ethic of the Scandinavian immigrant city. When I first saw them in the mid-1990s, the band embarked on fast-clipped, intensely coiled, and surefire melodic tunes that easily stirred the packed PIT crowd. Seeing Kalen onstage bolstered my sense that the scene had not buckled, not caved-in. People like Kalen had grabbed the reigns, for the better.

Sometimes, though, the most memorable nights occurred because gigs didn't happen as planned. "Mulligan Stu was on the bill with [snotty bumble-gum punk idols] Queers at the PIT," tells Kalen. "The Queers were *huge* at the time. The weird thing was that they were not on tour, just three shows in the Midwest. We went up to Green Bay to catch them

Trenchmouth, Alumni House

the night before our show. [The singer] Joe looked like shit! Sick as hell. They played and packed up and left right after the show. The next day in Rockford, the Queers were a no show. There were 900 goddamn people waiting at the PIT for the Queers, and they weren't coming! We ended up playing every song we had ever known. We might have stretched out to like an hour and fifteen minutes. That's hard to do with two and a half minute songs!" This was likely the pinnacle of punk activity in the area. In the 1980s, even hyperactive touring bands like SNFU only drew close to 300, so just as punk had spread through the globe like a virus via MTV, cheap CDs, fanzines in every city, and the beginning of the openly available Internet, it reached a kind of local zenith on nights like this, even when the Queers didn't bother to show up.

Other gigs became cemented in memory due to entirely different reasons. "I was hanging out at the Court Street house," remembers Kalen. "It was the On the Waterfront weekend, the Rockford Labor Day music festival." But this marked an odd occasion. "The Dickies were booked, a band we actually wanted to see!" Kalen enthuses. "It wasn't just the hackneyed classic rock band du jour for once. I made the lone trek over, since nobody at Court Street was interested. The temporary festival stage was somehow appropriately set up behind the Surf, a fairly seedy downtown strip club. I was hanging out, drinking some beers with some college-rock types when I noticed the distinct lack of punk rockers. There were a few of us ... but not the punk rockers en masse I expected."

A long line of punks left Café Esperanto, heading towards the infamous Los Angeles punk band. "I noticed out of the corner of my eye, across the State Street bridge, a virtual punk rock procession led by none other than the right reverend himself, Dwight Gail," a local legend supposedly ordained as a Universal Unitarian and known to flick firecrackers out his car window like they were chewing gum wrappers. "I saw them all in a single file line walk all the way across the bridge and file into the show. And the weirdest part is none of them said a word. There had to be like 50 of them! It was one of the coolest things I've ever seen at a punk show!" These temporary invasions of rather staid and bare downtown were rare at the time. Most gigs were clustered outside the dense but small urban strip, which often stayed mostly deserted at night.

On the southern fringe of Wisconsin, about a half hour from the avenues of Rockford, Beloit venues like C-Haus on Beloit College's campus, booked many Rockford acts, while The Hangout briefly stirred momentum by hosting bands as well, but Alumni House, a few miles away, quickly supplanted those by hosting regional acts and touring bands, including Plaid Retina, SNFU, and Trenchmouth (featuring Fred Armisen of *Saturday Night Live* and *Portlandia* on drums).

Rank, devilish hell-raisers the Scabs and A Bloody Mess ended a gig in an unsettling combo of Dionysian wreckage and vitriol, including a blowjob given by Bloody Mess to a surprised young fan that jumped on stage, which quickly irritated the soundman. Many consider this period of mayhem a low point for the scene. "The sound guy shut it down. He had enough," recalls Tom Williams. Bloody Mess, whose singer had been putting the mic up his ass, "started fucking with the guy. I remember I walked over and got in between them, and then the singer of veteran Milwaukee punk band 10-96 started flipping out. He threatened us, saying he had a gun. He lifted his shirt, and I saw the handle. People freaked and scattered. People screamed, 'Call the cops!' What happened after that is a blank. I do remember finding bullets on the floor." Co-promoter Dan Garrison wished he never booked it; both men were pissed about the stain of needless malevolence on a budding scene.

"Myself and a few other people like Jeff Weeter organized gigs, and Brad Towell and his band FLAC put on the first shows there since the post-war era," says Barb Orr. "Then, I left for Minneapolis, and other people took on the baton." DIY was the spirit that kept things manageable, hands-on, levelheaded, and democratic. "I'm not completely sure of the first show we booked at The Alumni, but it *always* involved Trenchmouth. Wreck from Chicago might have been the first headliner. Either that or Alice Donut, which was a fucking blast!"

Still, punk remained a far cry from its shouted mantra of gender inclusion. Nationally, the suburbanization of punk by the mid-1980s, often due to the success of bands like Suicidal Tendencies and Black Flag, increased the horde of barely teenage, testosterone-twitching, close-cropped hair men coming to shows. In turn, they too jumpstarted bands and pumped out bracing, often muscular hardcore that rarely flouted conventions or invented many new twists. Such adrenalized music often hooked men, yet repelled women, as slam dancing gave way to mosh pits and pigpiles. Hardcore became dude-saturated.

Still, women held on and joined, participated despite odds, and proved resilient: Melanie St. Claire penned reviews and shot pics of Flag of

Democracy and Henry Rollins, which I used for the cover of my fanzine *Left of the Dial*; Erika Grove hosted a Verbal Assault gig in her basement and went on to work at Lookout Records; and some women regularly attended shows and maintained social relationships within the scene. Still, the paradox of having a scene in which people robustly sang "Not Just Boys Fun" by 7 Seconds, but then often left women on the sideline, was acutely felt.

The gender dynamic improved markedly in the 1990s, as Orr proved, just as it did nationally, as if punk were finally re-aligning with the inclusive, zeitgeist-defining first and second waves of punk from the mid-to-late 1970s, when women would regularly be members of bands in New York, San Francisco, and England, often forming the backbone of the movement. Locally, by the beginning of the 1990s, Barb Stout sang in the fiery cover band Dodge Veg-O-Matic (unleashing covers of Blondie, Buzzcocks, and more), Marti Erickson sang for the semi-industrial/post-punk unit Bling, Jenn Weeter sang for hybrid modern punkers FLAC, and bass player Lynne Paulli anchored the rhythm section of an unnamed band inspired by the nimble roots-pop of Mike Watt's playing in fIREHOSE.

Whenever something DIY and underground was happening in the 1990s in Rockford, Matt Branch zealously wrote about it in his quirky zine *It's*. The front cover blurted, "More useless garbage than you could shake a stick at!!!!" in the left margin. "Don Cappy used to do a zine called *Betty's Rag*, and I was helping him with that. I had a crappy tape recorder, and we interviewed Not-Us at the Hangout. We were doing a lot of the cut and paste stuff. Suddenly, Don lost interest or wanted to do something else. So, I had maybe six or seven pages of stuff and didn't know what to do with it."

"People hanging out at Gary's did contribute," he acknowledges. "And I finally got sixteen pages together ... I didn't have the money to print it. I used to go to Denzil's Music Emporium ... and told [Denzil Showers] about the idea. He offered to give me $100 for a full-page back ad. Barb Orr drew it up. Later, I was supposed to pick up the ad and the money to get the damn thing printed. I was bicycling everywhere. I asked a few people for a ride to Beloit, but they were all partying at the time. I ended up getting frustrated and impatient and said, 'Fuck you guys. I'll ride my damn bike to Beloit. Can't be that hard.' Well, it was ... the first couple of times," revealing the grueling mileage on kneecaps.

"I made it up there and back, got the ad and the money. And somehow, I must have either gotten another car or maybe mine was in the shop at the time. I drove to Kinko's, talked with Tad Keyes, who made copies for me. [People] didn't think I'd ever pull it off. I got a little angry at my co-editor and pretty much said something like, 'Man, fuck you!' Now ... we gotta haul ass to Champaign, sell some zines, and hopefully interview Fugazi."

To make a video, Mulligan Stu partnered with high school peer Jim Fetterley, an indie/experimental filmmaker trained at the Art Institute of Chicago and Kartemquin Films. "A couple cases of Milwaukee's Best and we did all the filming in one night on Super 8 without much light," Fetterley confesses, "in a dark butcher warehouse wrapping feet and feet of linked sausage around Kevin's neck like it's a gold chain as he plays guitar and lip syncs. All colorized blue and yellow for effect because it was *soooo* underexposed."

He also directed local crossover metal band Sarkoma's "Troll's Opinion" video. "Singer Brian was nicknamed the troll. I shot pixelated Kodachrome 8mm in the basement and backyard of a house they were practicing at and in Brian's backyard and cut it with found footage with collaborator Rich. It kinda set us on our way with appropriation video for AnimalCharm. We did a Maya Deren-inspired short B&W piece with my roommate Rich, which we shot as our term paper for Film Noir class, then cut it with footage of the band partying. Somehow a shot of me wearing tanning bed goggles falling down the stairs ended up on a Sarkoma T-shirt! This video was way more mondo-garage-surrealist—both shot and edited in the early 90s—high grunge aesthetic, no digital editing, all film developed commercially, then DIY VHS transfers to be edited linearly shot-by-shot on JVC remote control.

"It's a little embarrassing to watch," he confesses, "but I like the overall energy. There were found films by our roommate and painter Jeremy Cook, found Halloween masks collection of performance video maker Erik Ullanderson, Fisher Price camera footage, and 8mm video of a Rotation Station show, 8mm film of Brian's backyard, and other textures." Needless to say, Sarkoma did not embrace the dissociative, wonky, and post-modern qualities as much as Fetterley, who still remains on the avant-garde film circuit today. For him, being a rust city rebel means exploring deep ties to the experimental past, not unlike Cleveland avant-garage rockers Pere Ubu.

Five
THE MILLENNIUM EXPLODES

Detractors will say that punk had an expiration date—the punk pendulum stopped swinging, even collapsed—and everything since 1982, or 1992, is no more than a simulation, a garden-variety ritual that is hollow, not hallow. But punk is renewed continuously, not retrograde, and still potent, not phony subversive. Punk history is tattooed on the music, look, style, and attitude of each successive generation, but those generations morph, according to their own codes and desires. As the Rockford hard-fought years melted into decades, the locations shifted, the music adapted, and the revolving door of personalities spun again and again, the community never stalled and crashed. Each generation sought, in its own way, to deal with the postindustrial aftermath—first the decimation of the 1980s, and then the partial, limited rejuvenation of the old city's fiber and spirit in the 1990s and 2000s. Punk was a way to witness, provide a stinging soundtrack as well as a combative narrative, and to cope with the rusting city.

As the Clinton years wound down, the city began to shed its industrial cocoon: many older industries closed up, but an extensive service industry thrived as the stateline suburbs filled with Chicago area commuters who sought the quiet, distant, often 'cookie cutter' bedroom neighborhoods near Rockford, which provided a lower cost of living. Medical branches cloistered around them; meanwhile, fast food seemed to spawn drive-thrus everywhere. Instead of being centered in Rockford alone, insurgent-cum-frenetic live music arose nearby in Belvidere and Roscoe, though a few new haunts in the dead-under-the-moon downtown district Rockford emerged too. It was a time for new blood as punk splintered into emo, third wave ska, dance-punk, post-rock, drunk punk, crust, and d-beat redux as the digital era bloomed. CDs, MP3, websites, and MySpace soon became the norm.

That One Place, a downtown Rockford venue, opened up shop right next to the old Times Theater. Running for about two years, it played host to a weird nest of gamers during nights when they weren't hosting shows. As Keelan McMorrow remembers, "They began life as a coffee shop, with a microwave on the counter and frozen things like corndogs and 'breakfast on a stick' that you could purchase and heat up yourself. Tons of local bands," McMorrow contends, "came of age in that spot. The Fightbacks were punk rock with a political bent. They're the only Rockford band who ever made it out to Gilman Street in Berkeley, as far as I know. Their singer, Meatball, was pretty active with his own label, 12MFA, and a succession of zines. They were a mainstay of That One Place era and epitomized DIY punk. They released one 7" EP, *Crybaby*, and one full-length, called *End of an Era*. The Fightbacks were part of Youth Against Hunger (YAH), a series of shows raising money and canned goods for shelters in Rockford. Magnum Opus was another band involved in these shows. A bunch of us would meet at Country Kitchen or Perkins restaurant to brainstorm ideas for YAH," including a compilation showcasing local acts appearing alongside bands like progressive Bay Area punks Fifteen as well as Chicagoans like Lawrence Arms and Alkaline Trio. "Meatball worked for years at the Kinko's [just like Tad Keyes and Chris Furney before him] on State, printing up stacks of flyers for free," McMorrow fondly remembers. "But one of the best acts of the era was Jeffy Checker and The Shizams. They performed an incredibly catchy blend of ska, jazz, and dub. Their frontman Jesus Correa went on to perform in a thousand other musical projects, even running for mayor of Rockford in 2009. Bassist Matt Ulery is pretty much a staple in the Chicago jazz circuit these days."

Gigs ended at the PIT skate-park, and That One Place lost its lease. Kids were restless, so a few resilient, DIY-minded people sought new places to fill their needs. According to McMorrow, "The all-ages scene kept up momentum with shows at the Lion's Den at Rockford College. The Bait Show and the Cabin were up in Roscoe Village/Rockton near the border with Wisconsin. They were cool DIY spots run by Elliot Porter. He drummed for the Moment, who were very reminiscent of [Omaha dark wavers] The Faint. They were really popular locally with a fan base that transcended the punk/subculture crowd. They put out some solid recordings and toured." The Cabin, though, became infamous. "Rob Biavati, who made gig flyers and helped with promotion, did one of his 'exhibitionist performances' when he stripped down in the lot outside the Cabin and ran inside during somebody's set, swinging from the rafters naked. I was encouraging him, of course. 'It's just a body', he'd say afterwards."

Rockton, barely a hiccup on the map, was a bedroom community that usually attracted quiet antique hunters. But for a few years, it became a molten epicenter of punk desires. During its peak, according to Porter, who practically lived in his grandpa's space, Outlaw Bait and Tackle, from 1999-2000, he booked gigs three to four times a week: "It used to have docks that were practically right out the back door. It was a small two-room place with white walls in the main area. There was a small, narrow back room with counter space where we usually put the band gear. The Cabin was also on the river, but in Roscoe. It used to be the clubhouse for a local snowmobile club back in the 70s."

But Rockford remained a bigger circuit than surrounding areas. "A coffee shop called The Divine Cup hosted shows from within the Salvation Army downtown. So did a small indie record store called Fifteen Minutes, located in the Highcrest Shopping Center," recalls McMorrow. "But some little old ladies complained about the 'weirdoes' congregating in the parking lot there after hours and it all got shut down pretty quickly. The Fightbacks were allowed to play shows in the HIS Cup show space, but they were not allowed to sell their *Crybaby* 7" because the cover art depicted an attempted suicide. The Legion Hall in Cherry Valley was a large space above the police station that had a good run. Unfortunately, that came to an end when my band, the Stellas, played a routine set, lighting our drums on fire and causing general mayhem.

"The Stellas was mainly forged out of the ashes of Third Degree Burns, a punkabilly band," McMorrow recalls. "They were all greasers at the time—pomade, cuffed jeans, patches on Dickies jackets. They played around in the late 1990s, and put together a Rockford compilation called *Screw City: More Factories Than Decent People* with local acts. They lived for a while in a house on Napoleon St., dubbed Napoleon House. Lots of parties happened there, sometimes shows in the basement too, which were packed to the walls with punks, greasers, and skinheads. They even held boxing matches down there for fun. Their singer Mario Panagiotopoulis [now a cinematographer in Los Angeles] was pretty busy studying film at Columbia in Chicago, and the rest of the guys were ready to try something new. So, I ended up on vocals, "Johnboy" Turner was on bass, and Jason Akin played rhythm guitar. Zach Medearis was our lead guitarist."

The Stellas invaded dismal downtown. "We started booking lots of shows at CJ's Lounge on the corner of State and Madison," says McMorrow. "Until well past 2005, on any given weekend, the place was packed with punks, scene kids, and onlookers, and underage kids rarely got carded. We even practiced in their basement for a while." They also played myriad basement shows—spaces that need no bartenders, no stage, no bullshit—including drummer Josh Moore's house located on 10th Street, later immortalized on the cover of the Fightback's album (Josh was their first guitarist).

Unfortunately, the Stellas' reign was short-lived. "Something burned us all out really quickly," McMorrow recalls. "My memories are a frenetic blur of drunken shows, insane parties, and fistfights. By 2001, we parted ways, and Zach, Jason, and Johnboy formed Thee Spokesmen, an excellent Billy Childish-inspired garage/power pop hybrid. I joined forces with three traditional skins from the Rockford scene. Jason Judd gave me a call about singing for a new project. Jason was the erstwhile guitarist for the reggae-tinged Shizams, but he wanted to go punk this time around. Chris Weber handled a second guitar, Mark Meyer wrangled the bass, and I brought along Josh from the Stellas to man the kit. We called ourselves Egan's Rats, after a prohibition-era St. Louis street gang." The cool name was in homage to regional history and outsider lore, something important to the band's ethos. "In contrast to the self-destructive debauchery inherent to the Stellas," McMorrow avows, "Egan's Rats was all about giving back and building something

... I started screen-printing our own shirts, so we could sell them ridiculously cheap at shows. A kid could buy a 7" record from us, a T-shirt, a patch, and a pin, all for under $12." The veins of Rockford DIY punk culture felt intact. Such bands offered something greater than momentary distractions, more than wild nights of puke and pugnacity.

A new era bloomed. "The scene experienced a renaissance ... Multiple punk shows were happening at different locations throughout the city on the same night, all of them well-attended," notes McMorrow. "A few times Egan's Rats even played multiple shows on the same day, all within Rockford city limits. PJ Heckinger from Carly's Day Out formed a transitory group called Cusack, later joining the Moment, and they became a force in the downtown scene playing Faint-style rock anthems with overdubbed sampling. Meatball,

the singer from the Fightbacks, formed Laydig with Paul Bourgeois of Uniform Pants. Around 2003, a group of guys appeared out of nowhere calling themselves Deadly Nightshade ... a sister-band to the Rats, playing a stunning, melodic style of punk rock with conscionable lyrics. We released a split 7" with Deadly Nightshade on my own Dirty Rat Records label, the follow-up release to the *Shanghaied* 7" EP by Egan's Rats."

By 2004, Rockford's fervid scene revitalized further. The Bollox featured adolescent Ryley Walker, now an NPR-featured folk musician. "They were kiddie punks, teenage kids, some of whom couldn't even drive yet," says McMorrow, "who grew up going to Egan's Rats shows. They played a poppy, sloppy style of pogo punk. An ongoing string of bands formed from the ashes of the Bollox: the Cavities, Boulevard Trash, etc." Overall, the scene simmered: The Cavities and Boulevard Trash and the Knaves formed; Hopes Anchor played emo-tinged hardcore; curiously soft and sincere emo-pop God's Reflex echoed Jimmy Eat World and released two albums—1998's *A Brief Lesson In Affection* and 2000's *Scenes From A Motel Seduction*—on Johann's Face Records, then morphed into The Braves; Albert Fish unleashed grindcore, the Gallows played metal; Chaos A.D. barked anarcho-punk; Vince Bucci retrofitted his Cherry Bombs into Vince and the Revolutions; former Apostles of Gein bassist Doug Sorg founded hardcore thrash/skatecore unit The Fibs; and persistent scenesters Mulligan Stu kept pursuing rust belt dreams.

"Tons of touring bands were coming through Rockford too," McMorrow remembers. "Hardcore legends M.D.C. made an appearance at a hippie joint called Minglewood that let us do the occasional punk show in their large patchouli-scented retail space, although things got strange when one of the hippies died in the back. P.J. Heckinger, who was in the pop punk Third Generation Mafia in the mid-late 90s, and Aaron Googe opened up a short-lived record store in 2003 next door to the Minglewood called Broken Down Records, which shared a space with a used-clothing company called Hunky Dories. So, shows began happening there too and some other fun things like spoken word nights. I once weirded out a bunch of kids by giving a lecture on bomb-making. I thought I was being funny, peppering the lecture with Irish-nationalist propaganda. Problems with finances and the landlord shut the place down. Googe later formed a not-for-profit community group that cleaned up waste areas around town before he relocated to the Pacific Northwest."

Activist punks, inspired by national zines like *Slug and Lettuce,* and any number of anarcho or progressive punk bands, "revved up a local Food Not Bombs chapter and distributed literature at shows, while a bunch of us began using bicycles as sole forms of transportation, making us easy targets for harassment on Rockford's car-happy roads," McMorrow laments. "I got chased by some guys in a truck once for flipping them the bird and ended up hiding inside the Irish Rose pub ... There were lots of people intolerant of bikes on the road for whatever reason. Everyone figured you were a loser or had too many DUIs." Plus, the city had been an extended part of the auto industry's backbone: it lacked bike lanes, lacked much of a liberal consciousness, and generally lacked much sympathy for day-to-day green modes of living, though a few years later nearby cities like Chicago became examples of 21st century eco-minded policies and thriving urban green movements.

As always, a brain drain similar to that of the 1990s dwindled the town's talent too. "Rockford's always had a difficult time," McMorrow avows. Blocks downtown started to become gentrified for "localvores" and epicure Asian cuisine. It used to be a mix of workaday world and hidden Bukowski-like poetry where one could spend Fridays in no-bullshit pool halls and devour cheap and greasy Greek take-out. Now, a different vibe set in. "One by one people were disappearing to Chicago and Minneapolis," just like the 1980s-1990s. The need "for jobs and changes in scenery stole a lot of us away. Meanwhile things back home began imploding, as bands broke up and shows became increasingly sparse. The PIT quit doing shows again for the last time, finally closing their doors completely in 2004. The Divine Cup guys were pushed out by their Salvation Army landlords, and they relocated to Detroit. Broken Down Records closed after a year. An indie spot called Acme Records opened on Broadway and Alpine and accommodated punk shows in-house, but the owner ripped off the bands and soon vanished. Friends got

sucked into bad drugs, some people died ... The Rats played our 'last' show in 2006 to a capacity crowd at the former Minglewood spot, then re-christened 'The Rockbox' and funded in part by Guzzardo's Music. The floorboards shook; we were actually afraid they would cave in. I think the final door count surpassed 400 kids." Soon, though, McMorrow jettisoned the town, exiling himself north.

The dislocation was apparent. "Exactly one year later, I had awkwardly begun adjusting to life in Madison, WI, which never really fit, so I soon hightailed it to Chicago. Our drummer, Scott, who'd previously replaced Josh Moore on the kit, got a call from Jerry Only of the Misfits," a world-famous horror punk outfit constantly promoted by Metallica and formerly fronted by Glenn Danzig. "Jerry Only hoped to set up a benefit show in Rockford. He wanted Egan's Rats to play it. Moreover, the whole thing was to happen at the Coronado Theater, Rockford's 'Crown Jewel' and a place where punk shows should never really happen. I thought the whole thing was a terrible idea. Of course, we told him we'd do it, emphatically."

The mysterious Misfits-Rockford connection was not a fluke. "For years, there had been rumors about the Misfits putting down roots in Rockford. I remember a guy called Tumbleweed showing up at a Stellas show at 10th Street, claiming to be a Misfits roadie. He had an ID card and band pass to prove it. He said he started out touring with the Circle Jerks back in 1981. He showed up with our friend Creepy, who'd been swearing up and down that Doyle, the guitarist for the Misfits, had married Gorgeous George, of wrestling fame and a Rockford native. She'd previously

been tied up with professional wrestler "Macho Man" Randy Savage. They were living in Rockford. By some weird twist of fate, Jerry Only had also ended up marrying a woman from Rockford, and his new father-in-law thought it would be a nice gesture if his band played a benefit gig for nFactor [for at-risk youth] in his wife's hometown."

"At this point, it's safe to say that the Misfits aren't what they used to be," argues McMorrow. "I worshipped the band as a teenager. I had the crimson ghost painted on my first leather jacket, and my mom made me a Misfits cake for my sixteenth birthday. But Glenn Danzig could really sing, his voice is iconic. He didn't sing for this incarnation of the group; in fact, by the time of the Misfits' Rockford performance, Jerry Only was the closest thing to an original member. Even [guitarist] Doyle had quit carrying out his role. Instead, the Misfits were composed of a hodgepodge of aging punk talent: Dez Cadena of Black Flag was on guitar and Robo was on drums."

The story unfolds like a reality-show script. "We met up in one of the Coronado's loading docks and towed in our equipment. We were given a quick tour of the theater's labyrinthine underground 'backstage' passages and ended up in our vast private dressing room, complete with illuminated mirrors and showers, [which were] bigger than most venues we'd played. We went upstairs to do our sound check on a stage that's supported Frank Sinatra, the Marx Brothers, and John F. Kennedy. Then it was upstairs for a pre-show meet and greet in one of the Coronado's pressrooms, enjoying cheese and crackers with a shirtless Robo and flash fan photography with Jerry Only. Outside the building, lines formed, and Jerry Only went to wave at the crowd and hail them with his presence."

Hi-jinx, letdowns, boisterous egos, and the drama of big time celebrity commingled. "Some punker kicked one of the glass entrance doors, it shattered into a million pieces. By the time we finished our set, I could barely breathe. I wasn't used to having a stage that big to run around on. I went backstage and bumped into [Cheap Trick guitarist] Rick Nielson. He shook my hand and told me something about '...us rock stars.' Everything's about as strange and surreal as it can be. The Misfits were absolutely terrible that night. Jerry Only can't sing to save his life ... Between songs, he pontificates to the crowd, blowing hard about all of the incredible work that he's done; the great things he's still doing. Some kids spit at him: he challenges them angrily. 'Nobody spits on Jerry Only!' he exclaims. He tells people to be careful with the seats, 'they're antiques.' I met him backstage later on. He gave me a great big bear hug. He does this to everybody, and he's not such a bad guy in reality. He genuinely wants people to like him, and he's accessible in a way few other performers are. Still, that old mystique is crushed: the demented brain-eating ghoul with a devilock is an embarrassing and overbearing dad chaperoning at the prom. We all ended up at a party in an old apartment of mine later that night. The new tenant had caught a squirrel with a trap in the crawl space. We fed it snacks and named it Jerry."

CONCLUSION

The stories of McMorrow, myself, and all the others illustrate the struggle of Midwest kids attempting to forge an underground community in a place where dime-a-dozen jobs at tool and die machinist factories dried up and the medical centers coped with an influx of cheap heroin deaths, gun wound victims, and a population with an exploding waistline. As feisty youth and angry adults, we didn't shrink away from making music, whether in a cold-entombed basement or a bar where the regulars would rather punch you than pogo. As corporations attempted to strip away our dignity in low wage conditions, people tried to erase local history, parents tried to make kids conform to the Bible, the media proffered outdated, whitewashed media stereotypes, and schools pretended that radicalism was a dead spirit, punk gave us the means to question, resist, and change those perceptions. Youth of Today guided me towards vegetarianism, M.D.C. as well, whose singer Dave Dictor, now a close friend, molded my politics and humor. But early on, I was a child of David Bowie; literally, a tiny kid wandering through the Martian landscape of same-samey ranch homes, fast food fiberglass, and corn strewn flatlands, lucky to have Bowie spur my consciousness. We can all be heroes, he told us. And I still believe that.

Rockford underground kids still exist as a cross-section of rebels inheriting the ethos, diligence, and spirit of the IWW types. Though those tough-minded immigrants from the early 1900s fought diligently for One Big Union and a justice-enshrined worker's world, we tried to create a close-to-the-ground, participatory, youth-centered democracy within the shell of the old; we too created a new history on the spot as the trains clambered by, the buildings looked gap-toothed from neglect, and normal people stared thick with indifference.

Sure, not everyone shared my liberal-left leanings. Not everyone supported the Human Rights Campaign Fund and the Nature Conservacy; wrote or signed letters to the Senate, Congress, The Secretary of Defense, U.S. Dept. of Justice, parole boards, departments of corrections, and major corporations in an effort to impact policy and decisions; not everyone became student activists breaking into the regents meeting of a college; not everyone joined the Young Socialist Alliance and Progressive Student Alliance and penned letters to the New Unionist; not everyone broke local laws handing out meals for Food Not Bombs or organized fundraisers for sick punks, the Red Cross, and gay rights organizations. But I did for decades. For that reason, I feel that Rockford punks are connected to our IWW brethren. Without my local punk community impacting my views, habits, and group skills, I might have chosen different fights.

I left, went West in 1993, became a writer full-time and buried myself in the lingo of books and teaching. Still, I always know others lived just as boldly, just as creatively, purposefully, and witty, back in Rockford, which spat me out like a time-bomb, ready to rework the world. In their own way, in their own time, other kids sought, and still seek, their own righteous paths.

Rust never sleeps. Neither do punk kids caught in a fray.

SUBSCRIBE TO EVERYTHING WE PUBLISH!

Do you love what Microcosm publishes?

Do you want us to publish more great stuff?

Would you like to receive each new title as it's published?

Subscribe as a BFF to our new titles and we'll mail them all to you as they are released!

$10-30/mo, pay what you can afford. Include your t-shirt size and month/date of birthday for a possible surprise! Subscription begins the month after it is purchased.

microcosmpublishing.com/bff

...AND HELP US GROW YOUR SMALL WORLD!

...and check out our other fine scene histories: